RESPONSES TO THE

RESPONSES TO
THE GREEN PAPER

Edited by
PETER GOODWIN and WILF STEVENSON

BFI PUBLISHING

First published in 1994 by the
British Film Institute
21 Stephen Street
London W1P 1PL

Copyright © British Film Institute 1994

British Library Cataloguing-in-Publication Data.
A catalogue record for this book is available from
the British Library.

ISBN 0-85170-429-8

Cover design: Romas Foord

Typeset in 10/11½ pt Sabon by
Goodfellow & Egan Phototypesetting Ltd, Cambridge

Printed in Great Britain by
St Edmundsbury Press,
Bury St Edmunds, Suffolk

Contents

Introduction

This book has the seemingly simple purpose of presenting in easily digestible form the range of formal responses to the Government's November 1992 Green Paper on *The Future of the BBC*.

The apparent straightforwardness of the task is deceptive for two reasons: the first is a feature of all such exercises, the second specific to this particular one.

Any selection inevitably implies judgments as to what is significant and what is not. Our aim has been to tease out of the responses the issues which are likely to prove important in the current debate on the BBC. We make no apologies for that. But it does have as its inevitable corollary that those who have raised issues which are marginal to that debate – however valid they may in the end turn out – will feel neglected.

This particular debate presents a special problem. For reasons we try to explain in our next chapter on the political background, it is a debate which has some notable elements of consensus. Many of the questions asked by the Green Paper have evoked a remarkable unanimity of response. We have tried to record that consensus clearly, but thought it sensible to devote most of our account to recording the areas where there is still substantial disagreement.

Two further editorial observations are worth making. Again, the first is general, the second specific to this particular debate.

The process of formal response to government consultation papers is never even an approximation to the full discussion. Much of the most pointed debate goes on in the press or in professional forums. Many of the organisations which do respond are clearly going through the motions, maintaining their institutional profile before government. And a number of players, who quite clearly have something to say on the question at issue, for one reason or another simply do not submit a formal response. So, for example, in the current debate, neither BSkyB, the Liberal Democrats nor the Adam

Smith Institute submitted formal responses to the Green Paper, although all have made substantial presentations of their views, on at least some of the issues at stake, in other places.

We have tried to take this into account. In our background comments, introductions to issues and linking comments we have tried to acknowledge the debate taking place outside the channel of formal responses. That said, we must stress that the main task of this book is the limited one of giving a flavour of the formal responses to the Green Paper.

Finally, the great degree of current consensus in the discussions on the BBC, both in formal responses to the Corporation and in the wider debate, should not be allowed to pass without comment.

The absence of proposals from the radical free-market Right is surprising. Little more than seven years ago a government-appointed commission, the Peacock Committee, highly influenced by the free-market think-tanks, unanimously recommended subscription funding and a Public Service Broadcasting Council as central to the long-term future of the BBC. Today both proposals have been quite marginal to the debate on the Green Paper. Equally, public service broadcasting today may have a lot more friends than might have been expected five years ago, but it is nevertheless striking that not a single one of the responses to the Green Paper proposes a qualitative *increase* in public provision.

The Background

The BBC was granted its current Charter in 1981; it expires at the end of 1996. Scarcely had the current Charter started than the future of the Corporation was once again up for debate. That debate has continued ever since but the parameters of discussion have altered, both with changes in the broadcasting environment and shifts in political mood.

In its early years the Thatcher government took two major decisions on broadcasting which were to have an indirect but profound effect on discussion on the BBC a decade later. It established Channel Four and thus for the first time brought into being a significant independent production sector in British television. And it adopted the recommendation of the 1982 Hunt Report that cable should be developed in the United Kingdom wholly by private enterprise. The BBC itself abandoned plans to participate in direct broadcasting by satellite a few years later. Thus by the mid-80s the Corporation was effectively excluded from major participation in the development of the two new delivery technologies.

In the first half of the 80s direct Government attention to the BBC's future focused on the funding of the Corporation. Spurred on by reports from influential free-market think-tanks and by lobbying from the advertising industry, the Thatcher government seriously considered the possibility of funding the BBC at least partially from advertising. With this approach in mind, it set up the Peacock Committee on the funding of the BBC in 1985. The Peacock Report, published in 1986, was perhaps the high-water mark of a free-market thinking on the BBC, and both its approach and many of its specific recommendations were to prove enormously influential. The exact pattern of influence was however a complex one.

The Peacock Committee interpreted its brief very widely; it felt that it could not deal with the funding of the BBC in isolation from the rest of the broadcasting environment and made recommendations right across broadcasting.

3

Peacock came out firmly against advertising on the BBC for two reasons. There were not sufficient extra advertising revenues about, and, in a situation where there were only a limited number of channels, competition for advertising would lead the channels to become increasingly alike, thus diminishing programme diversity, and therefore reducing consumer choice.

The fact that a committee dominated by free-market economists came out with such a conclusion was decisive. In practical political terms it killed the idea of advertising on BBC television stone dead. If the responses to the Green Paper are anything to go by, there is no sign of its resurrection.

Peacock's positive proposals did, however, envisage a long-term and fundamental change in the funding of the Corporation. He divided likely developments in broadcasting into three stages. In the first stage new channels would develop but most viewers and listeners would continue to rely mainly on the BBC, ITV and independent local radio. During this stage the BBC would continue to be funded from the licence fee which should be indexed to the general rate of inflation. In the second stage, as new channels and methods of payment became established, BBC funding would shift from licence fee to subscription. Finally, with an indefinite number of channels and pay-per-view and pay-per-channel readily available there would be a full broadcasting market.

Peacock argued that even this full broadcasting market would leave a need for public service broadcasting, funded by public money. It recommended that as from Stage 2 this public money should be dispensed by a Public Service Broadcasting Council giving grants for specifically public service programming on all channels, not just the BBC.

The Government adopted the Committee's recommendation on indexing the licence fee. But Peacock's longer-term subscription-based strategy appeared to find little favour in Government circles. The idea of a Public Service Broadcasting Council has been specifically floated in the current debate but, as we shall see, it has had few takers outside the Government, which itself seems distinctly luke warm about the proposal.

It was Peacock's recommendations in the non-BBC areas of broadcasting that were to have the most influence on broadcasting policy. Among other things, Peacock recommended that the ITV franchises should be auctioned and that Channel Four should sell its own advertising. In modified form both of these proposals were incorporated in the 1988 White Paper on the Future of Broadcasting and the 1990 Broadcasting Act.

4

One further important Peacock recommendation, applying to both ITV and BBC was also implemented by the Government – a quota of television programmes to be made by independent producers. Peacock had suggested a quota of 40 per cent to be implemented over ten years. The Government settled on 25 per cent, to be implemented rather quicker, first of all as a recommendation and then by law in the 1990 Act.

One other more general aspect of the Peacock Report's influence should be noted. The report focused heavily, and for the first time in British public debate, on the question of the economic efficiency of broadcasters. That focus has coloured debate on the BBC ever since.

In the aftermath of the Peacock Report Government attention shifted away from immediate major changes in the BBC and towards the commercial sector of broadcasting. Neither the 1988 White Paper nor the 1990 Act contained much about the BBC. The White Paper said that the BBC 'will continue as the cornerstone of public service broadcasting. The Government looks forward to the eventual replacement of the licence fee, which will however continue for some time to come'. The only major provision in the 1990 Act concerning the BBC was the 25 per cent independent production quota.

The BBC may have largely escaped legislative changes after Peacock, nevertheless some major shifts were taking place in the Corporation as a result of Government policy.

By indexing the licence fee to the general level of inflation for three years from 1987, the Government exerted a 'double squeeze' on the finances of the BBC. The base at the beginning of the three years was significantly less than the BBC had wanted, and costs in broadcasting are generally considered to rise faster than the general rate of inflation. In 1990 there was a further squeeze. For one year the licence fee increase was to be 3 per cent less than inflation. The Government's financial pressure on the BBC since the mid-80s has reinforced focus on measures to increase efficiency within the Corporation.

In the early and mid-80s the Thatcher government had a number of confrontations with the BBC over programming issues, and was widely seen as being particularly hostile to the then Director-General of the Corporation, Alasdair Milne. In 1986 when the chairmanship of the BBC's Board of Governors became vacant, the Government appointed Marmaduke Hussey. Shortly afterwards the Governors dismissed Milne, appointed Michael Checkland as Director-General and brought in John Birt as his deputy, initially with special responsibility for news and current affairs. Birt succeeded Checkland as Director-General at the beginning of 1993.

The new regime at the BBC has been characterised by fewer rows with Government over programming, a more interventionist approach in day-to-day matters by the Governors, and by a concern to reduce staff numbers. In 1991 Checkland unveiled the policy of Producer Choice, which came into operation in April 1993. Producer Choice effectively establishes an internal market inside the BBC, and opens that market up to outside competition.

One result of the shifts in BBC management style and approach since Hussey's appointment has undoubtedly been to make the Government less antagonistic to the BBC, as a supposed bastion of spendthrift liberalism, than it was even a few years ago.

Improvements in BBC/Government relations have also resulted from developments on the Government side. The proposed reforms of commercial television in the 1988 White Paper were considerably softened by the time they reached the statute book in 1990, and further softened when they were implemented by the Independent Television Commission. Even so, the 1990 Broadcasting Act found very few friends outside Government circles. That poor reception in the industry, coupled with numerous problems arising from implementation, seems to have diminished Conservative enthusiasm for further major reform in broadcasting. The departure of Margaret Thatcher in November 1990 must have added to this retreat.

The result is an enormous contrast in tone between the way the Government in the Green Paper of 1992 has approached the BBC, and the way four years before it had approached ITV. In the 1988 White Paper the Government simply unveiled a series of radical reforms to a generally hostile industry and public. The tone of the 1992 Green Paper could scarcely be more different. One newspaper leader aptly described it as 'long on options, refreshingly short on recommendations'. David Mellor, who as broadcasting minister piloted the ITV reforms through Parliament and, as the founding Secretary of State for National Heritage, presided over the first drafts of the Green Paper, has gleefully warned his colleagues about the dangers of listening to 'glinty eyed pamphleteers'.

Increasing convergence in policy between the Government and BBC management has not taken all the heat out of the debate on the Corporation's future. In the lead up to the Green Paper there have been a number of attacks from prominent figures in broadcasting on the new regime at the BBC, alleging authoritarian management style and expressing considerable doubts about the policy of Producer Choice. Among the more notable have been those by Channel Four chief, Michael Grade, veteran BBC India correspondent, Mark Tully and playwright, Dennis Potter. The new regime was also subjected to particular criticism shortly after the publication of the Green Paper, with the revelation that incoming Director-General, John Birt, had spent his five years as Deputy Director-General as a service provided by his own company rather than being on the BBC staff. This arrangement was agreed by the Chairman and Deputy Chairman of the Governors, and the controversy over it has fuelled more general concern about the role of the Governors.

The convergence between the Government and the new regime at the BBC is reflected in both the Green Paper and the BBC's *Extending Choice* published a few days later. It also sets the framework for the responses to the Green Paper which are analysed in the rest of this monograph.

First there is a core consensus among respondents on three key issues – in favour of the licence fee, in favour of maintaining the present range of the BBC's television services, and against a public service broadcasting council. This consensus would not have existed five years ago. We outline it in our next chapter. The amount of space that we devote to the few responses that disagree, should in no way detract from the strength of the consensus.

Second there is a series of important, but clearly delineated, areas of controversy. These areas of disagreement are outlined in our next twelve chapters, which form the bulk of this book. They are the BBC's commercial activities, the Corporation's approach to the non-English nations and the English regions, the scope of radio services, independent production and the policy of Producer Choice, the definition of public service broadcasting, the role of the BBC's Governors, the accountability of the corporation to the licence payer, the rest of the broadcasting environment, equal opportunities, the possibility of privatising BBC transmission, the level and method of setting of the licence fee, and the legal framework for Charter renewal. These twelve areas of controversy are, we believe, likely to form the meat of the debate over Charter renewal. In some cases we have cited responses on these issues at considerable length, because we feel the detailed views expressed are likely to figure prominently in that debate. It should be noted that on several of these major issues of controversy – for example over Producer Choice and the role of the Governors – it is the present BBC regime, rather than the Government, which bears the brunt of pro-public service criticism. Finally, it is inevitable that respondents should focus on issues of particular concern to themselves and therefore that some important issues should be raised by only one or two organisations. These may not figure so prominently in the debate. They may nevertheless be intrinsically important. So in our last chapter we record some of the more significant of these other issues raised in response to the Green Paper.

The Core Consensus

Introduction
1. The Green Paper asks a wide range of generally very open-ended questions about the future of the BBC. On three major issues raised by the Green Paper the respondents display overwhelming consensus:

- They are for maintaining the current scope of the BBC's television services.
- They are for keeping the BBC funded by the licence fee.
- They are against the introduction of a Public Service Broadcasting Council as a dispenser of public funds.

The Scope of the BBC's Television Services
2. The consensus on maintaining the scope of the BBC's television services is so overwhelming that it can be summed up very quickly. *Not a single response* calls for the BBC only to have one television channel. *Only one response* comes near to suggesting that the BBC withdraw from 'popular' or 'entertainment' programming and confine itself to a narrow highbrow definition of public service. This is the response from the Institute of Practitioners in Advertising:

The IPA believes that the next BBC Charter should:

Enshrine the new BBC commitment to focus on television and radio programming activities which genuinely extend choice, and only address needs which commercial broadcasting may not fully meet and to assign priority to the truly distinctive rather than to quantity of output. ...

The IPA believes that the policy objectives set out in 'Extending Choice' are a positive blueprint for a coherent programme strategy vis-a-vis the commercial sector. The difficulty comes, however, when translating the objectives into practical day-to-day decisions on programme planning and commissioning. The IPA believes that this is the nub of the problem for the Department of National Heritage to address.

For example, what precisely are 'the areas where there is a strong public need which commercial broadcasting may not fully meet'? What is 'real choice, not more of the same'? Clearly difficult qualitative judgements are required, but the IPA feels that a specific and actionable remit must be established for the BBC if the laudable policy objectives of the BBC 'Extending Choice' booklet are to be achieved in practice. ...

The IPA also believes that the BBC, in fulfilling a role which is complementary to that of the commercial sector, should refrain from scheduling competitively against ITV (e.g. transmitting a popular film at the same time as another popular film on ITV). In its privileged position of being funded by the licence fee, the BBC should not feel compelled to wage a 'ratings war' against ITV, but should schedule its programmes in a way which extends viewers' choice. This has a further advantage for advertisers who will thus be able to access larger audiences for popular ITV programmes. (Institute of Practitioners in Advertising, 4.1, 4.6, pp. 7–8)

3. Against this, response after response expresses the wish that the BBC continue providing television programming across the full range. Perhaps most significantly such a position is clearly asserted by the BBC's main competitors in terrestrial television, ITV and Channel Four. In direct answer to the Green Paper question as to whether the BBC should continue to broadcast a wide range of services appealing to all tastes and interests, or concentrate on programmes unlikely to be provided by other broadcasters, ITV replies tersely:

The public is best served by a wide range of services. One of the stated purposes of Government policy is the extension of choice: it would therefore be perverse if the BBC were to reduce the range of its services as new ones come on stream. (ITV, 7, p. 19)

4. Channel Four is just as supportive:

Commercial channels will invest in programming up to a level sufficient to achieve the audience required to attract revenue – but not beyond. In countries where public service television is weak, usually for financial reasons, then the overall range and quality of television is poor. But where you have strong, public service television channels, driven to produce excellent, home-grown programming of all kinds for their domestic audiences, then *all* television has to aspire to the same quality in order to compete and gain share of viewing.

For this reason it is important that the BBC continues to broadcast a wide range of services across two channels, appealing to all tastes and interests and competing with all terrestrial networks. It would be no service to the viewers to confine the BBC, for example to programmes of minority interest only, or to force it into a cultural and educational ghetto. The support of the BBC for popular comedy shows like *Last of the Summer Wine, One Foot in the Grave*, or *Only Fools and Horses*; for mainstream drama series like *Casualty*; and for sports like Motor Racing and Tennis is just as important a part of public service broadcasting as the transmission of classical music, adaptations of major novels or news and current affairs etc.

These popular quality programme strands have three important functions. First, they have high production values and do not underestimate the audience – thus setting standards for other UK broadcasters. Secondly, they are British produced programmes, commissioned for a British audience and thus they are an important support to the British production industry. Thirdly and most importantly, they bring pleasure to millions of viewers. The BBC's record in comedy, most particularly, has never been equalled by commercial television. (Channel Four, 2, pp. 1–2)

5. As can be seen in the section that follows on public service broadcasting, a number of responses take the BBC itself to task for neglecting popular programming. The formulations in *Extending Choice* cited above by the IPA are specifically criticised by several other respondents as making concessions to a 'narrow' interpretation of public service broadcasting. With the exception of the IPA there is no equivalent criticism of the BBC in the other direction.

The scope of the BBC's radio services evokes a more varied response. Although a clear majority of respondents seem to be in favour of maintaining all the current services, there are some significant respondents who propose reductions in scope. We deal with this debate in our section on radio.

Funding the BBC
6. The consensus on retaining the licence fee as the method of funding the BBC is almost as overwhelming as the consensus on the scope of BBC television services. However, it is not quite unanimous.

Only two organisations submitted responses opposing the licence fee. One was the fringe right-wing Freedom Association:

The licence fee system offends against two principles. The first is that, like the poll tax, it is set at a flat rate regardless of ability to pay. ... Secondly, there is no provision ... for persons to be exempt from the levy if they wish to view only commercial television. ...

... the Peacock Committee has already concluded 'that in the longer term subscription should replace the licence fee as the main source of BBC finance'. ...

... this opportunity ought to be seized to introduce some equity and logicality into the present bizarre and indefensible system of financing. (Freedom Association)

7. The only other outright opponent of the licence fee is the Cable Television Association, the trade association of the British cable companies. It too argued for subscription:

The Peacock Committee suggested that subscription should replace the licence fee as the main source of BBC finance. Bearing in mind that by the end of the decade 25–30% of the population will be subscribing to cable television, and that research shows that BBC1 accounts for 25% of viewing in those homes able to receive Astra channels, compared to 33% of viewing in all TV homes, we believe that subscription would certainly be a fairer system of charging consumers.

With regard to the cost of the present television licence, we feel that although '22 pence per day' sounds like value for money for BBC programmes, cable television customers pay an average of 38 pence per day for 30 or more channels although they have to pay the additional 22 pence per day for BBC programming whether they use the service or not. (Cable Television Association, p. 3)

8. Alongside these two outright opponents of the licence fee three other organisations express support for supplementing the licence fee either by sponsorship or by advertising. Independent television producer, Mersey Television, strictly limited its advocacy of advertising to Radio 1:

For Radio One, advertising could provide a way of keeping culturally in touch with the age-group it is supposed to serve. Sponsorship and advertising are a way of life in pop music – it would not sit uncomfortably with the station's place in popular culture. It would also have the incidental benefit of generating additional revenue. (Mersey Television, 18.iv, p. 11)

11

9. The other two organisations which were willing to contemplate advertising or sponsorship on the BBC were both directly involved in the business of advertising. The Incorporated Society of British Advertisers was unconditional in its advocacy:

> Advertising should not be rejected or belittled as something which is broadly disliked by viewers, and which is of no concern to the BBC. The facts do not bear out these assumptions, and the Government should not close the door on the possibility of the BBC benefiting through advertising income.
>
> The Government should accept the principle of a mixed funding approach, including some methods by which advertising and sponsorship can be included in BBC income, in order to maintain high standards in BBC programming. We believe that viewers will increasingly resent paying the licence fee, as their viewing to other channels increases, while their viewing to the BBC declines. All other major countries in Europe now have fixed funding for state channels, with advertising a major source of income.
>
> Viewing patterns will change substantially over the next decade, and the BBC TV share (with 2 channels) is likely to drop to 35% or less by the year 2000.
>
> Without a mixed funding approach for BBC TV, its income will increasingly fall below the rapidly growing cable and satellite subscription income, and the buoyant advertising income of ITV/C4/C5.
>
> Similar principles should be applied to BBC radio, with a mixed funding approach, but the effect on BBC finances will be small.
>
> A joint venture format on one channel, or a complete separation through 'subletting', especially in peak time, could achieve the necessary funding on BBC TV.
>
> The potential growth in TV advertising, and its value for business activity and competition, as well as a way of funding programmes, is still substantial.
>
> The ISBA does not accept the argument that a small diversion of advertising income (perhaps £300 million by the year 2000) to BBC TV would unbalance or unfairly affect ITV, Channel 4 and other commercial services. (Incorporated Society of British Advertisers, p. 1)

10. The Institute for Practitioners in Advertising was (virtually alone among respondents) in favour of sponsorship on the BBC, but altogether more cautious about advertising:

The BBC already has experience of dealing with sponsorship through its broadcasting of sponsored events. Programme sponsorship would be a natural extension of this involvement.

Commentators are generally agreed that the quality of programme sponsorship to date on ITV has been good, with no evidence of editorial influence. Agencies and advertisers have worked hard to ensure that the sponsorship messages appearing on screen have been of a quality sympathetic with that of the programme material. ITV programmers also clearly have a vested interest in achieving this effect.

The evidence so far available on programme sponsorship suggests that a large proportion of broadcast sponsorship funds (probably over two-thirds) are new money to television and not money withdrawn from spot television advertising. BBC involvement in broadcast sponsorship should therefore have a minimal disturbing effect on the spot advertising revenue market.

Although the ITC sponsorship code could be used as a template, the IPA believes that any sponsorship activity undertaken by the BBC needs to be distinctive and compatible with the BBC's image. The broadly educational role of many BBC programmes could preclude them from being appropriate sponsorship vehicles. The IPA feels that the BBC might wish, initially at least, to select perhaps between six and 10 television programmes for sponsorship, representing a diverse group of target audiences e.g. in the areas of arts, sports, weather, drama and light entertainment. BBC arts and sports programmes are seen as key areas for sponsorship.

It would also be the case that monies provided for BBC sponsorships would go back into programming for the benefit of the whole viewing public and not to the bottom line for the benefit of shareholders as could occur in the commercial sector.

The IPA estimates that limited programme sponsorship, along the lines outlined above, could provide the BBC with in excess of £10 million per annum at current prices. (It is estimated that television broadcast sponsorship in total attracted approximately £15 million in 1992.) Though a relatively modest income source in the BBC's accounts, it could in time represent a sizeable sum in the context of budgets available for funding the arts. ...

The IPA also suggests that the option of advertising on BBC core services should be kept open, as in the present Charter, so that, if circumstances were to warrant it, the Government could give its assent to advertising at some point in the future if, for example, Channel 5/6 was not launched or if the BBC departed from its currently recommended programme policy remit which the IPA proposes should be enshrined in the new Charter. (Institute of Practitioners in Advertising, 4.7, 4.11, pp. 8–10)

11. The case for retaining the licence fee and against advertising was made in far too many responses to give even a representative selection. We will quote just two:

We feel strongly that it would be a serious mistake to put the BBC into competition for revenue either by requiring or allowing it to raise funds from advertising, programme sponsorship or subscription. All international experience shows that such a shift to competitive funding would change the BBC out of all recognition. It is true that Channel 4 is operating, so far successfully, as a public service broadcaster with commercial funding. The introduction of Channel 4 in 1982 and its subsequent growth has met the pent up demand for more air time for sale. That demand is now satisfied. If the BBC were required to be funded commercially, competing for both audiences and revenue with ITV, it would be in the same position as companies like the Dutch broadcaster, NOS, or CBC in Canada. In both these cases the gradual introduction of advertising has meant a perceptible and continual dilution of the 'public service' content of the schedule, as the extent to which both companies have been required to compete for revenue with other advertising financed mainstream channels has increased. Their experience shows that the BBC programme service would inevitably be forced into the narrow mass market. Thus the extent to which it was able to invest in distinctive or risky programmes would be severely curtailed, thus reducing viewers' choice.

Further, putting the BBC into competition for revenue would also have very serious, direct *economic* consequences for the rest of commercially funded UK television.

It is argued by those who support advertising on the BBC that advertising spend has grown faster than GDP for over a decade and that an increase in supply would create extra demand. However, it is difficult to see the justification for such bullish views.

International experience is mixed and therefore hardly supports the case of the enthusiasts for commercial funding. For example in France and Italy it is true that deregulation did lead to substantial increases in total advertising expenditure and in television's share. But the same pattern does not emerge in Japan or in the United States in the last 20 years, despite large increases in the number of channels available. Channel 4 would therefore argue that it would be too great a risk to introduce *any* element of commercial funding, whether from advertising or sponsorship, into the BBC. It would threaten not only the programme service the BBC could offer viewers but the commercial future of the rest of UK television. (Channel Four, 5, pp. 3–4)

The ITC agrees with the findings of the Peacock Committee, which, as the Green Paper suggests, are reinforced by more recent studies, that the total television advertising market is not capable of funding the BBC as well as independent television. The Green Paper draws attention to the position in which Channel 3 licensees who bid for their licences in 1991 would find themselves if advertising were to be allowed on the BBC. But advertising on the BBC would also imperil the future and independence of Channel 4, restrict severely the continuing development of the satellite and cable industry and rule out any realistic prospect of an advertising-financed fifth terrestrial channel. The likely outcome would be either a proliferation of inadequately financed services with a reduction in range and quality delivered to viewers, or the concentration of television into the hands of a few dominant suppliers, or both. ...

The ITC is therefore firmly opposed to advertising in any form at all on the BBC. Sponsorship is a close substitute for advertising in specific segments of the advertising market. The ITC considers that the BBC's concerns about the influence of sponsors are exaggerated, but agrees that sponsorship within the scope of the BBC's present practice, which is confined to the coverage of sponsored sporting and artistic events, is likely to remain only a very marginal source of income. The ITC's firm view is that the BBC's use of sponsorship must remain within its present limits for the same reasons that lead it to oppose advertising on the BBC.

Similar arguments apply to subscription income in relation to general interest as distinct from specialised services.

The BBC do not themselves favour subscription as an appropriate mechanism for funding their core services, and the Commission agrees with this assessment. A broadly based public system on a subscription basis would reduce its 'reach', and a significant proportion of viewers would be deprived of services which they now enjoy. The competition for audiences which is offered to the commercial services, which is important for sustaining programme quality, would be significantly more limited than in the case where services are free at the point of delivery.

The ITC's view is that the BBC's television services should continue to be funded in future, as they are now, from the licence fee. Although the licence fee has been much criticised, it does provide, particularly under the present indexing arrangements, a stable form of income which is consistent with the purposes and objectives for which the Commission believes the BBC should be aiming. It is difficult to see that any other form of public funding, such as an annual subvention from the Exchequer, whether or not paid for nominally out of the Government's income from the Channel 3 licensees, would provide as secure and independent a basis for future development of the public service. The Commission can see no reason at present why the licence fee should not continue, provided the 'reach' of the BBC's television services is maintained, for at least another 10 years. (ITC, 39–43, pp. 10–11)

A Public Service Broadcasting Council
12. The Green Paper asks 'should there be a Public Service Broadcasting Council either to regulate the BBC or to promote, finance and regulate public service broadcasting by the BBC and other services?' The formulation of the question is somewhat confusing. As introduced into discussion on broadcasting policy by the Peacock Committee, the expression Public Service Broadcasting Council meant a body giving *grants* for public service programming – *not* a regulator. This is the way most respondents have taken it. A few have simply borrowed the term to refer to proposals for restructuring regulation of the BBC. We touch on these in our later sections on the Governors and accountability.

In its commonly understood grant-giving sense, the Public Service Broadcasting Council finds *only two* takers among respondents. Only one of these supports it in the sense proposed by Peacock:

> The Cable Television Association would support the setting up of a Public Service Broadcasting Council to promote public service broadcasting, and to be responsible for financing public service broadcasting. We would endorse the view of the Peacock Committee that one of the purposes of such a Council should be to ensure separate and secure funding for programmes of merit

16

which would be unlikely to be broadcast if a number of channels, including the BBC, were competing for audiences and for finance.

Cable operators are obliged under their licences to provide public service broadcasting in the form of local programming. Cable operators also provide other services such as educational programming and ethnic programming and we believe that if funding for such programmes was awarded on merit, this would enhance and promote high quality and diversity in these areas. (Cable Television Association, p. 3)

13. The other supporter of a grant-giving Council has a radically different conception of its source of funds:

We are not in favour of the licence fee being siphoned off for a new 'National Arts Council of the Airwaves'. The BBC already carries that mantle through the licence fee.

However, there is a case for looking at the ITV licence fees, amounting to £300m p.a., which we believe could be successfully channelled to such a broadcasting arts body if a special levy were to be made on those companies which returned low bids to secure their licences. This would also level the ITV playing field, as well as providing more funds for broadcasting.

All terrestrial channels should be made to allocate specific airtime for public access programming funded by the National Arts Council for the Airwaves.

This proposal should be considered in relation to the BBC's place alongside other publicly funded arts bodies, specifically the regional arts bodies, as there is probably considerable scope for greater co-operation in this field. (Mersey Television, 19 i–iv, p. 11)

14. Against these two are ranged virtually every other respondent. Again, it is particularly telling that the other terrestrial broadcasters – who would in theory be the likely beneficiaries of such a Council – oppose it. ITV says simply that it 'does not support the idea of such a Council' (ITV, 7, p. 21). Channel Four presents the following case:

Channel 4 does not support and sees no benefit whatsoever from the concept of a Public Service Broadcasting Council. Even though we might be thought to be one of the main beneficiaries of such a funding system we believe it would inevitably bring politicians and bureaucrats closer to decisions about individual programmes than is healthy in a democracy. Committees do not, as a rule, make good decisions about difficult and highly subjective creative matters. Crucially we do not believe it will encourage ITV to carry 'public service' television programmes. The important issue for ITV when considering which programmes to transmit is not simply the cost of production but the rates they can charge for air-time – low audiences for mass appeal channels (like Channel 3) mean lost revenue which a programme subsidy from a Public Service Broadcasting Council could not make up for. We can find no argument that a PSBC would improve the quality of programmes on offer to the viewers. Quite the reverse. It also risks impoverishing the BBC. It is simply a rotten idea. (Channel Four, 6, pp. 5–6)

15. Among the many other responses opposing the concept of a Public Service Broadcasting Council, one other is particularly worth singling out. The concept is sometimes described as 'an arts council of the airwaves'. The real Arts Council, however, has this to say about it:

We do not support the idea of a Public Service Broadcasting Council. Any attempt to move towards separation of the BBC's public service and other commitments is likely to discourage a coherent and mixed approach to broadcasting.

The Green Paper acknowledges the danger of conferring significant financial power on one organisation. There is also the danger that such a system of public funding would also by default lead to a narrowing of the range of programmes, removing arts programmes from the broad programme mix in which they flourish. (Arts Council of Great Britain, 6, pp. 12–13)

The BBC's Commercial Activities

Introduction

1. Alongside its core activity of public service broadcasting largely funded by the licence fee, the BBC has from its earliest days engaged in commercial activities like publishing *Radio Times*. The Corporation now has a wholly owned subsidiary, BBC Enterprises, which runs a range of commercial activities with the stated object of supplementing licence-fee income. In recent years some of the BBC's commercial practices have come under attack from the Monopolies and Mergers Commission (MMC) as anticompetitive. For example, the MMC ruled against the Corporation's monopoly use of BBC programme listings in *Radio Times*. At the same time the Corporation has started a number of radically new commercial ventures. It has taken a part share in a UK-aimed satellite channel largely programmed with repeats of BBC drama and comedy, UK Gold. And, after having failed to secure government funding for a television equivalent of World Service Radio, the BBC has launched World Service Television (WSTV) as a self-financing venture, funded by advertising and subscription in partnership with a number of commercial broadcasters around the globe.

The extent of the BBC's commercial activities has aroused considerable controversy which is well represented in responses to the Green Paper.

2. Several respondents, representing very different constituencies, questioned the whole range and philosophy of the BBC's commercial ventures:

> The role of BBC Enterprises ... poses important questions. If the BBC is to start serving a world market might this not lead to a constrained representation of British society? There is clearly some conflict between the BBC's 'international' ambitions in television

and its domestic role as national broadcaster, as well as those which stem from its recent involvement with the market-place through UK Gold, for instance. We reassert that serving a British audience, in all its diversity, must be the BBC's priority and, though some commercialisation is a necessity, it is not and should never be the BBC's core activity or purpose.

More investment in British television drama or British film, for instance, to avoid the inevitable complications of co-productions, will necessitate either a higher licence fee or a reduction in output. But without this, there will inevitably be suspicion that the more the BBC depends on international co-production funding the less central will be its commitment to British cultural diversity and to British audiences. If any commercial opportunities are sought they should never imperil the BBC's public cultural remit. (British Film Institute, pp. 5–6)

The BBC's commercial activities demand energetic scrutiny. While BSAC recognises that the BBC should maximise the value to the licence-fee payer of the monies it receives, it is concerned that, with BBC Enterprises, the Corporation has occasionally wandered a long way from its core activities with little to show for it in terms of additional revenue for programme-making. Of equal concern is the suspicion that the BBC may be in businesses in which it does not properly belong, either because these could be amply undertaken by the private sector or because the BBC is inhibiting or distorting competition by its behaviour. These issues are highlighted by UK Gold, which makes of the BBC a commercial satellite broadcaster, a status decidedly at odds with that on the basis of which it enjoys a monopoly of a compulsory licence fee.

BBC Enterprises is a function of a philosophy which took hold in the 1980s that the BBC should be seen to be behaving entrepreneurially. It is not necessarily the case that Enterprises' activities have consistently contributed to the BBC's bottom line, nor that it has made the most of the revenue-generating potential of such BBC resources as its programme archive.

BSAC attaches great weight to the BBC's pledge to operate its commercial activities within a clear framework and to relate these activities to the BBC's core commitment while ensuring that they consistently produce a return for the licence-fee payer. These criteria must be strictly adhered to and continually demonstrated. Against this background, BSAC believes that the government, or a parliamentary committee, or a re-vamped Board of Governors, should take a rigorous look at the BBC's current and proposed businesses and be satisfied that they do indeed fall within the parameters which have been set. In the most significant area of the exploitation of programme rights, it must be ensured that the BBC's arrangements are conducive to the long-term interests of licence-fee payers and that there is not a hint of a dog-in-the-manger attitude on the part of the Corporation which, while unable to realise the full value of those rights, might be preventing others from doing so. (British Screen Advisory Council, p. 4)

We are interested in the suggestion developed in the BBC's paper 'Extending Choice' that the Corporation will seek to earn an increasing proportion of its funding from commercial activities.

We question the propriety of the BBC using its privileged position as a publicly funded Corporation to launch, for example, satellite services which will compete for audiences and revenue with other commercially owned ventures be they advertising or subscription funded. It would be more appropriate for the BBC to concentrate its activities and energies on the service it is funded to provide – terrestrial television and radio and world service radio – licensing out, where appropriate, to existing alternative suppliers the development of commercial spin offs.

We believe that the BBC should fully exploit the value of its programme catalogue, but that programme sales should be conducted in a market open to all bidders, rather than the BBC transferring rights to related parties such as UK Gold, without seeking other offers. We do not believe that the BBC is fully realising the revenue potential of its considerable programme assets. (Channel Four, 4, 8, pp. 6–7)

The BBC is not a brand name like any other, but is an important national institution which has received heavy investment from licence payers over the years. Although the principle of delivering commercial services as a means of raising extra finance for BBC core activities is hard to question, this must be done in a way that does not compromise the BBC's very unusual position.

It is not clear that this message has yet been properly absorbed.

More fundamentally, activities of this kind raise a number of questions about how the BBC links up with private-sector companies whose main concern will be to maximise the returns to their shareholders. This arises both in the context of publications – as for example with the partnership with Redwood for the publication of consumer magazines – and in relation to programmes, e.g. in relation to the BBC's link with UK Gold for the provision of subscription services, and its deal with BSkyB over football broadcasts. Can such links be consistent with the maintenance of the BBC's independence and promotion of the highest standards of public service? How do they relate to the BBC's policy of refusing all advertising? What implications do they have for universality and access of the BBC's output?

A further worry arises from the market for programmes and programme making. International co-productions are a growing part of broadcasting, and this may well be of direct consumer benefit if the end results help to promote the principles of variety, range, diversity and quality. ... However, it is important to recognise the limits to this process. Three issues arise in particular:

(i)   The BBC must be wary of becoming so reliant on new markets for its programmes that it deliberately focuses resources on programmes designed to be sold abroad, from the outset. This would involve trading the direct interests of UK consumers in programmes designed to meet their needs against potential profits from the world marketplace. The need to meet the BBC's UK objectives is and must remain paramount.
(ii) Licence-payers' funds may be used as start-up capital for commercial ventures not intended mainly (or at all) for a UK audience.
(iii) As with the case of BBC publications, there is a risk of the BBC's name being misused where programmes are produced purely for commercial purposes, i.e. for resale to commercial broadcasters – such programmes may well be made to different standards from those the BBC would apply to its own output. Using the BBC name may also put independent producers of programmes on an unfair commercial footing in both the preparation and broadcasting of their programmes, given the BBC's high level of recognition, both among audiences and among those whose cooperation is needed in the production phase. (Consumers' Association, pp. 4–6)

The ITC believes that the BBC should not be allowed to compete indiscriminately. Its commercial activities should be confined to turning to account the assets needed for its core broadcasting business, as for example with the night-time subscription service which it is already providing. The BBC should of course not be prevented from selling rights in its programmes to the providers of, say, a commercial satellite service or to other commercial services either at home or abroad. The BBC should not be permitted, however, to use broadcasting expertise or resources funded out of the licence fee to support, develop or promote commercial activities in ways which result in competition on an unfair basis with other wholly commercial organisations, whether at home or abroad. The ITC considers that, as it appears the disqualification provisions in Schedule 2 of the 1990 Act were intended to ensure, a line should be drawn at the BBC's participation as a financial partner in a commercial television service, whether financed from advertising (as is UK Gold at present), sponsorship or subscription. BBC World Service Television should not be to any degree a charge on the licence fee payer. (ITC, 26, p. 7)

3. Other (although fewer) responses put a more positive view of the BBC's commercial activities:

While BBC Enterprises will never be able to generate enough income to fund the public service broadcasting activities of the BBC, its activities have been of real benefit to the BBC and the licence payer. It does however make a significant contribution and BBC programme schedulers would be severely limited without the money generated by BBC Enterprises Ltd.

In the mid to late 1980s the BBC was encouraged by government to maximise its commercial activities. It now appears to be criticised by government for its success. It would be strange indeed if BBC Enterprises had not gained advantage from its close association with the corporate BBC, and it is through this relationship that BBC Enterprises has developed new and significant markets.

In so far as is possible, BBC Enterprises should continue to operate as the commercial arm of the BBC, providing its activities are consistent with and supportive of the concept of public service broadcasting. (BECTU, 5, pp. 10–11)

4. However, BECTU also added two major qualifications:

Not all the activities of BBC Enterprises have been in the interests of public service broadcasting. We are particularly concerned about the development of UK Gold, a service funded by public service broadcasting, but only received by those with satellite dishes. BECTU is equally concerned about the arrangement between the BBC, BSkyB and the English Premier League which removed coverage of live football from the remit of public service broadcasting. We cannot foresee any circumstances where such arrangements are in the best interests of the viewers and listeners. (BECTU, 5, p. 11)

5. A different type of positive response was to be critical of BBC Enterprises current performance, but to encourage it to fulfil its commercial potential:

> PACT [Producers' Alliance for Cinema and Television] believes that, judged on purely commercial terms, the BBC has failed to properly exploit the value of its output across the different media that make up the secondary sales market. For example in the year to March 1992 the contribution of BBC Enterprises to BBC income was a £1.7 million loss whilst the investment made by BBC Enterprises in new BBC programming was probably no greater, and may even have been less, than the gross profit from overseas programme sales.
>
> BBC Enterprises should therefore be given a period of time within which to match its performance to the commercial sector or it should be shut down and the exploitation of BBC programmes in secondary markets be assigned to commercial distributors who can maximise revenues. The BBC would benefit directly in the revenues accruing from this strategy which could be ploughed directly back into the Television Service.
>
> The BBC should maintain a policy of exceptionally taking ownership stakes in other broadcasters – like UK Gold – which offer further opportunities for a paying public to see *Porridge* or *The Good Life* whilst generating extra revenues to be ploughed back into new programming.
>
> The BBC's commercial framework for dealing with independent producers has also failed to make the BBC the first port of call for independents with new programme ideas. The BBC's existing policy of acquiring all exploitable programme rights militates against independent producers being able to provide better developed projects to the BBC at a lower cost. The BBC should therefore adopt a policy of acquiring limited transmission rights from independent producers and where appropriate shifting the costs of development back into the independent sector. (PACT, 5, pp. 11–12)

6. At least one other respondent was positive about both the BBC's commercial record and its commercial future:

> We see no objection to the BBC supplementing its licence fee income from commercial enterprises which exploit the public appeal of its programme output and in other ways. However extensive these commercial undertakings might become, in realistic terms the vast bulk of the BBC's income will continue to be

derived from the licence fee as long as the present system of funding the Corporation remains. These commercial enterprises are therefore not likely to compromise the public service basis of the BBC as a broadcasting organisation. Nevertheless, we would urge the Government to specify that commercial aims must consistently underpin and not dominate the achievement of the quality objectives inherent in a public service.

BBC Enterprises has developed into an effective multi-headed commercial undertaking operating in a variety of different markets. As a publisher, BBC Enterprises is an efficient and well-run organisation. In particular, the company is one of a number of publishers which has negotiated a minimum terms agreement with the Society in respect of its published output.

BBC Enterprises is intent on developing the market for audio cassettes, in which it is currently market leader. In this field the company's record is less commendable, and a minimum terms agreement for writers whose work is exploited by the BBC in this way has yet to be negotiated. Meanwhile, the pernicious practice of buying out some writers' copyrights continues. We would urge the Government in drawing up a new Royal Charter to require BBC Enterprises to conform consistently to the highest commercial, as well as creative, standards in its operations. (Society of Authors, 6.6–6.8, p. 7)

UK Gold, WSTV and publishing

7. Individual commercial operations of the BBC singled out for particular criticism were UK Gold, WSTV and publishing activities:

The BBC is not consistent in its attitude to advertising in 'Extending Choice'. It argues forcefully that even a partial reliance on advertising would be damaging *for its core services*. The implication is that advertising would be acceptable on non-core services, though it does not say what they are.

The BBC does however indicate its belief in 'mixed funding' as a way of raising supplementary income. This includes 'participation in subscription television'. It does not say whether or not this should exclude participation in channels which are in part funded by subscription and in part by advertising.

Yet already the BBC has a 20% stake in UK Gold, a satellite channel which carries advertising. In April there was a press report that the BBC is planning three further satellite channels, all funded by advertising.

ITV believes the BBC should follow the logic of the principle it asserts so clearly in connection with the licence fee: it is the only form of funding which gives it 'freedom from the commercial pressures to maximise audience ratings and share' ('Extending Choice'). Even indirect involvement with advertising-funded channels will erode this freedom bit by bit.

The new BBC Charter should prohibit any such involvement.

ITV does not believe the BBC should use either the licence fee or any of its secondary revenues to take part in risk ventures.

The licence fee liberates the BBC to pursue its core objectives. It is wrong per se for the BBC to get involved in activities which could undermine its ability to achieve these objectives.

Further, not only does the BBC run the risk of losing money (as it could be doing on UK Gold), but it diverts BBC management from its proper task of delivering the BBC's own services as effectively as possible.

Indeed the only obvious beneficiary of the BBC's involvement in UK Gold is the US cable company, Cox, which has in effect been given a subsidised entry into the UK broadcasting market, by being able to exploit the BBC's programme library – originally paid for out of licence fee money.

Nor should the BBC seek to find other ways of taking part in such ventures, e.g. through bartering its programmes for equity. Whatever secondary value resides in the BBC's programmes should be realised in the way we describe in Section 2.4.

The next BBC Charter should prohibit any kind of participation in commercial ventures in the UK. (ITV, 2.2–2.3, pp. 7–8)

A report last year prepared for the Commonwealth Relations Trust on 'Developments in 24 Hour Television News in the United Kingdom and Europe' concluded:

> While it [WSTV] is supposed to be a commercial operation, it is not considered profitable on its own, and appears unviable without the support of the BBC. The BBC provides WSTV with spare production capacity in its television facility free of charge, the use of its radio and TV reports, and access to the BBC library of current affairs material round out the WSTV schedule. The cost of producing the service is unclear and so is WSTV's revenue. Sales figures are not public and the fee is believed to vary greatly between markets. Free trial periods are believed to have been offered as incentives to some companies to pick up the service.

While we cannot vouch for the accuracy of these claims they, nonetheless, reflect and echo ITN's very real concerns. It seems to us that BBC World Service Television is funded directly or indirectly by:

(i)   commercial revenues such as the payment from Star TV;
(ii) tax payers' money in the form of the grant from the FCO to World Service Radio whose resources are being used in part to service World Service Television;
(iii) licence payers' money which is paying for BBC news operations for viewers in the UK which are being used to provide resources for World Service Television.

The public has a right to know where its money is going. We recommend, therefore, that an independent audit of BBC World Service Television should be carried out as a matter of some urgency to establish, among other things, the conditions under which international contracts are currently being pursued. (ITN, p. 2)

8. Some contributors, however, thought that the solution to the WSTV dilemma was for the Government to fund it:

World Service Radio is well established, highly regarded and separately funded. It should remain as it is. World Service Television is currently entrepreneurial and funded in a complex manner resulting in an untidy intrusion of commercial messages and some consequent diminution of editorial purity. We fear that WST, looking increasingly for commercial funding, will not easily sustain the claim of full independence – the hallmark of World Service Radio.
   The Media Society recommends that the Government should consider actively helping to fund World Service Television. (Media Society, 5, p. 2)

9. Others were enthusiastic about WSTV continuing on its present course:

As regards World Service Television, no less than 94% of respondents to our questionnaire endorsed the proposition that the BBC should strive to make international broadcasting a significant and money-earning element in the future. There was a feeling that the infant BBC World Service Television, even within the commercial environment in which it is currently operating, has already achieved a successful format and approach while preserving essential elements of the BBC World Service from which it derives, and keeping alive the sense of the BBC image. (Society of Authors, 5.14, p. 5)

... the magazines and other products sold by BBC Enterprises seem to be becoming increasingly remote from the idea of the BBC as a broadcasting organisation which should *'pursue single-mindedly ... public service roles and objectives' (Extending Choice*, page 62)

One example of the apparent divide between policy and practice comes from the BBC's preparation of books and cassettes in support of its language programmes (a point noted in para. 4.7 of the Green Paper on page 19). This is laudable so far as it goes, as it clearly helps to promote some of the BBC's central objects. However, current advertising practice in this area seems far more geared to the use of the BBC name as a means of promoting sales than to promoting the basic objectives. For example, a recent BBC Enterprises advertisement for language learning courses (e.g. as published in the *Guardian* Weekend Section, 24 April 1993, p. 25) carries the BBC logo prominently, but 'BBC Enterprises' are mentioned only in the small print. This might be acceptable if the advertisement was mainly promoting a new BBC series, or providing details of supporting materials for such a serious stop. But no radio or television programme is mentioned, and this appears to be a purely commercial initiative. We seriously consider whether the use of the BBC's name and logo in this way is consistent with the purpose the BBC has identified for itself in *Extending Choice*. (Consumers' Association, p. 5)

Regions and Nations

Introduction

1. *Extending Choice* asserts that 'if the BBC is to inform national debate, express British culture and entertainment, and educate its audience, it must have a programme making and broadcasting presence across the regions of the UK'. It goes on to state that the BBC's regional broadcasting priorities should therefore be:

- To commission and make network programmes right across the United Kingdom.
- To deliver an authoritative local and regional news and current affairs service on television and radio.
- To invest in a high level of information, cultural and entertainment provision for Scotland, Wales and Northern Ireland.

As part of the commitment to produce network programmes across the United Kingdom the Corporation has established 'centres of programming excellence' for particular genres in Bristol (Natural History and Features), Manchester (Religion, Sport, and Youth and Entertainment) and Birmingham (Drama, Multicultural and Leisure).

A large number of respondents to the Green Paper are, however, deeply critical of both the BBC's past performance and sceptical about its future commitment in this area. To greater or lesser degrees the BBC is accused of being London-centred, delivering a metropolitan-biased culture and neglecting the rest of the English regions, Scotland, Wales and Northern Ireland. Scarcely any respondents leap to an unconditional defence of the BBC here.

2. A general case is put by the British Film Institute:

> The necessity for the BBC to reflect the nations, regions and geographically and linguistically linked groups in Britain is

29

paramount. Not only do the BBC centres in the nations need greater autonomy – financial and organisational – but the English regions have to be adequately served too. There is understandable ambivalence in Scotland, Wales and Northern Ireland about television's window on their distinctive cultures.

This is part of a larger argument about the nature of the British state and the role of the metropolis as a cultural centre. We note that the Government has recently issued proposals for devolution of responsibilities in the arts, and other spheres, and we note the obvious parallels for the BBC.

It is clear that in many respects the ITV system is becoming more centralised. It is therefore important that the BBC should have regard to its regional responsibilities. The growth in news and current affairs specialisms at the expense of other programme areas in regional output must be reconsidered so that the skills base and expertise in all programme areas can be maintained outside London.

This is not to say that local news and current affairs programming is not valuable. Indeed, there is a strong case for network broadcasting of more programming of all sorts produced outside the London metropolitan area. It is not a question of sending entire programming units to work in regional cities, but of creating opportunities for writers and producers to work in the regions in which they live. Production in the national and English regions should be neither pushed nor allowed to fall into the ghetto of folksy regionalism but seen as an opportunity to create high quality programmes of national and international interest from a non-metropolitan perspective.

In achieving a less metropolitan and centralising approach it is important that the BBC forge close co-operative links with cultural organisations, major funders and other groups, which represent the diverse make up of contemporary British society. (British Film Institute, pp. 3–4)

The Criticisms
3. A number of responses present statistics to drive home the extent of neglect of the regions and nations:

81% of the BBC's network programming is produced within the M25 ring. The BBC has made a commitment to increase production outside the M25 ring from 19% to 27% of its programmes. A welcome step but hardly sufficient.

TAC [Association of Welsh Independent Producers] believes that an equitable geographical spread can be achieved through the

30

operation of a competitive internal market in the BBC. We anticipate that there would be considerable resistance within the BBC to the establishment of such an internal market. In view of this we believe that the BBC were right to set themselves a quota. A quota of 27%, however, is totally arbitrary and manifestly too low. TAC does not have the information to propose a level but over a specified period of time, and given a level playing field, the distribution of production throughout the United Kingdom should develop to reflect the geographical distribution of the population. (TAC – The Association of Welsh Independent Producers, 3.8–3.9, p. 5)

BBC Scotland television produced only 4.4% of total network transmissions in general programmes in 1991/2. It is not possible to produce expensive programmes, such as drama, without a commitment from the centre, i.e. the network. Scottish voices do not have a clear access to the network with the result that the BBC is less Britain speaking to the world, and more London speaking to the rest of Britain. (Scottish Arts Council, 3.4, p. 3)

4. Far from having deepened its regional commitment in recent years some respondents criticise the BBC for having weakened it:

The NUJ believes that the BBC has a unique and crucial role to play in both radio and television in both the English regions and the National regions of Wales, Scotland and Northern Ireland and is therefore concerned at the cutbacks in these areas over the past few years. The replacement of the concept of Manchester, Birmingham and Bristol as truly network production centres with the concept of the three locations as so called 'centres of excellence' focusing on narrow specialisms with scant resources is a retrograde step.
    The English regions should reflect the nature of their communities across a range of programmes both for their own regional audience and the network. The National regions should also have the means in both television and national regional radio to produce programmes in English for regional consumption and for the network as well as programmes in the Gaelic tongues. As with the wider BBC, the NUJ welcomes the commitment to news and current affairs in the regions but would add the same qualification, namely that news and current affairs cannot stand in isolation in regional broadcasting and that it must be a part of a broad mix of programmes that cater for the needs of the audience and reflect the traditions, and culture of the region. (National Union of Journalists, p. 5)

5. One common point of emphasis is the importance of resourcing an improved regional production base:

> It is necessary for the BBC to continue to offer a comprehensive service to viewers throughout the UK. This means a full range of programmes addressing the specific concerns of viewers and listeners outside London and the South East, both in the national regions (Northern Ireland, Scotland and Wales) and throughout England. The regional programming commitment is key to the BBC fulfilling its public service role. Equally important, the BBC should draw on the country as a whole for its national, networked programming. This means maintaining significant production capabilities across the country.
>
> The need to maintain and extend the scope of the BBC's regional resources outweighs the demand for the greatest efficiency and cost-effectiveness. For the BBC to honour its commitment to programme-making in the regions, it must be able to resource regional activity properly. BSAC believes that the benefits of regional investment by the BBC extend beyond the BBC itself to the whole economy, culture and self-image of the regions and sustains the creative professions upon which the audio-visual industries depend. (British Screen Advisory Council, p. 3)

6. Criticism of the BBC's alleged regional failures falls into two parts, lack of regional input into the British broadcast network and inadequate regional broadcasting. Most critics take up both strands. But at least one response draws a clear distinction between the two:

> The Media Society believes that the BBC networks are too heavily representative of the South-East. The BBC should endeavour better to reflect the whole of UK society to all the viewers and listeners.
>
> Programmes designed for regional and local television viewers should continue but take a lower priority than those promised by the new Independent Television licences. (Media Society, p. 2)

7. Much of the criticism of the BBC's metropolitan bias comes from Scotland and Wales, but at least one response singles out the English regions as having particular problems:

> Some of the English regions have larger populations than the national regions. They do not, however, have comparable resources, nor do their advisory councils have similar responsibili-

ties to the national councils which are represented on the BBC's governing body. Consideration should be given to ways in which the role of the English regions can be strengthened. Regional opt-outs to supplement the regional daily news and magazine programmes on BBC1 should be provided, and should be adequately resourced. (Church of England Communications Committee, 12, p. 3)

Proposed Solutions

8. Although the criticism that the BBC is undercommitted to the regions and nations is clearly widespread, the solutions proposed vary. One major English regional independent producer presents a radical shopping list:

(i) Network location.
   One meaningful step to signal that greater priority would be given in future to non-London activities would be to take the 'centres of excellence' theory a stage further and establish a network headquarters – radio and television – outside London. This would provide an appropriate centre of gravity for all non-London activities.

(ii) Relocation of Radio Five.
   We would like to see Radio Five given greater focus as a channel for young people by developing non-London production. As a long term proposal, we would like to see the channel based outside London, working alongside the Youth programming department in Manchester, in order to provide for the young audience a cultural alternative to other London-based national channels.

(iii) Identity of BBC2.
   Implicit within our comments is the belief that BBC2 should remain an innovative channel – based on fresh regional initiatives. Credibility for this aim could be achieved by relocating the channel's key editorial and creative functions – such as scheduling and commissioning – to Manchester. (Mersey Television, 28.i–iii, p. 16)

9. The Association of Welsh Independent Producers, however, are altogether more sceptical about the value of moving offices out of the capital:

TAC does not consider that the transfer of whole programme departments from London to centres such as Manchester is the answer. Metropolitan programmes hosted by centres outside London will hardly reflect the cultural diversity of these islands. Real, organic centres of excellence, rather than artificial and synthetic ones would develop in the regions were the regions given a level playing field on which to compete with the London programme departments. As programming decisions are made by the London departments there is a vested interest in keeping production within the M25. (TAC – The Association of Welsh Independent Producers, 3.11, p. 6)

10. A number of other responses take up the issue of whether or how the BBC's regional 'centres of excellence' can be built upon:

The new 'Centres of Excellence' policy is in itself a mark of the BBC's internal recognition of the need for change, the need to shift some investment and resources away from the South East; there is more than one centre, and some of them are even north of Watford. But as both concept and practice these centres seem to be too much based on the missionary impulse to send talented and experienced southerners out into the nether regions; setting up new colonies to reflect the values and structures of the fatherland. They seem not quite to recognise that there may be excellence there already, indigenous skills and qualities capable of giving as well as receiving.

One weakness of the Centres of Excellence policy is that they have been conceived of as necessarily large and therefore also necessarily few in number; a second weakness may be seen to derive from too strong an orientation back into the world and culture of broadcasting (at worst the culture of 'HQ'), not outwards into a wider world and diversity of cultures.

Some of the best, most imaginative and most robust policy initiatives come out of the creative 'bricolage' of pulling together apparently disparate elements of good practice, and combining them into a new and vibrant whole. If we combine the organisational strengths and economies of scale possible in an institution funded by over twenty million licence payers, with a new devolution of power to the regions and nations (and appropriate forms of governance to ensure this), and a new advocacy of *small* production centres, we can begin to see a new organisational shape emerge – that kind of purposeful metamorphosis that is renewal.

Such small centres, like the nerve endings at the fingertips, might act as the most sensitive point of contact with a larger world, relaying their ordinary and extraordinary messages back to the brain; signalling an organisational openness to change and providing one additional and innovative mechanism for managing the processes of feedback and accountability.

These centres, widely spread throughout the nations and regions, might also encourage and facilitate the formation of a wider set of partnerships with, for example, national Arts Councils and Regional Arts Boards, bridging the old chasm between the broadcast and live arts, and situating broadcasting itself as a form of art, of popular cultural expression, within its regional context. (Sheffield Hallam University, 5.2, 5.5, 6.1 and 6.3, pp. 9–11)

Traditionally ... the BBC has concentrated on local news and events at the expense of local culture and entertainment.

This imbalance should be corrected by providing additional resources for non-news regional opt-out programming.

PACT believes that the most obvious way for the BBC to continue its commitment to regionally oriented network programmes and expand its commitment to local non-news output is to orient itself as a geographically devolved organisation – both in terms of management and infrastructure.

This would enable the BBC to more adequately reflect the diversity of the nation it serves, as well as to take advantage of cost savings available outside London and the South East and to provide jobs in areas of increasing unemployment. At present the 'Regional Centres of Excellence' for the production of network programming do not really assist the BBC region in which they are based except to increase the turnover of hotel keepers who house BBC staff seconded from London to work on particular programmes.

PACT believes that the proposed BBC policy of 'Proportionality' is a useful corrective to the existing metropolitan bias of the Corporation. In theory the creation of a Regional Broadcasting Directorate also represents a sensible basis upon which to further develop a regional production base so long as it is predicated upon the commissioning of programming which reflects the culture of the regions concerned rather than simply providing a series of 'warehouses' for production. (PACT, 4, pp. 6–7)

11. In Wales and Scotland there are some strong pleas for devolution of the BBC's decision-making structure:

... the Welsh Language Board believes that the BBC in Wales should have a far greater degree of autonomy to fulfil its obligations to the viewers and listeners. Whilst it is appreciated that its document 'Extending Choice' re-enforces the commitment to supporting the cultures of 'national regions', it is clear from that document that the preferred infrastructure for the BBC is centralist and London based. Authority and control in Wales rests with a directorate of regional broadcasting and accountability is through the centre. This does not square up with the development of other UK institutions. Government, economic planning, cultural investment, education, health, environment, housing and many other facets of life in Wales have been devolved and are autonomous in their decision-making process. By the middle of this decade, unless there is a radical reconstruction of its organisation, the BBC will not be accountable to its viewers and listeners in Wales in any real sense. (Welsh Language Board, 3.7, p. 5)

In the light of concerns for the future development of Gaelic through television and the need for a dynamic relationship with Gaelic radio, the Committee would recommend that BBC Scotland should receive a much greater degree of autonomy in the future structure of the BBC.

It is important that the BBC maintains its editorial independence, and the Committee has respected this principle in all its discussions with the BBC. At the same time, in the interests of the audience and to expedite effective strategic planning, it seems appropriate to recommend that a formal link be established between the Committee and the BBC's governing Council in Scotland, either directly or through its Gaelic Advisory Committee.

Based on the principles of autonomy, accountability and editorial independence and the evolution of a more direct relationship between the BBC in Scotland and its audience, it is recommended that BBC Scotland should have control in Scotland over one of the two terrestrial television channels managed by the BBC, probably BBC2, whilst playing an active part in the overall UK and international service provided by the BBC. (Comataidh Telebhisein Gaidhlig, 7.5–7.7, p. 9)

12. Although there is scarcely any opposition to more regional input into the BBC's network, there is some opposition to the BBC getting into or staying in some more local services:

... the ITC does not believe that BBC and commercially funded services should be merely mirror images of each other in terms of functions. The BBC should not be permitted to develop new types of service simply because the commercial sector does so. An example would be local or city-based television services, in competition with those which are already developing, for example, on some cable services. The BBC should be required to contribute to maintaining competition and choice at national and regional levels, where its strengths based on public funding are best deployed, and where the core audience for television is bound to remain. (ITC, 23, p. 6)

Radio

Introduction

1. The debate about the range and nature of the BBC's radio services is likely to prove rather less of a formality than the equivalent debate about television. Whereas there is no challenge whatsoever to the BBC retaining two television channels, a significant number of respondents question whether the BBC should retain all the radio services it delivers or intends to deliver:

> The [Radio] Authority recognises that cultural and educative programming should ideally be folded into an attractive format so that it avoids an elitist label. But it questions whether six national channels (i.e. Radios 1 to 5 and the projected 'all-speech' channel) are necessary for the BBC to accomplish its task. (Radio Authority, 27, p. 10)

> In radio we feel that the distribution of frequencies is very uneven. Why should the BBC have five national FM services while the independent system is confined to one, with a further two using discarded BBC AM frequencies? The BBC can surely discharge its public service obligations with a maximum of four services. (Radio Clyde Holdings, pp. 8–9)

Radios 1 and 2

2. The respondents who advocate some pruning of the BBC's range of radio services are however less certain and united on what particular services they would like to see the BBC withdraw from. Some point a questioning finger at Radio 1, but are uncertain what the effect on the advertising market of its privatisation might be:

> As regards national radio, our conclusion is that the only service likely to be provided to the same extent by the independent sector is Radio 1. ...

The balance of argument for and against transferring the Radio 1 frequency and format to the independent sector is a complex one. ... In essence, a judgement of the effect of adding a Radio 1-type service to the present gamut of Independent Radio services rests on whether there would be a decisive and positive effect on total radio advertising revenue, such as to enable a commercial Radio 1 and other commercially-funded services to thrive; or whether strong competition from a Radio 1 format for a not greatly increased total radio share of advertising revenue would drive down rates and threaten the viability of other services. The Authority would not feel confident that there would be a tonic effect if the change occurred now (which is of course not in question). So much is likely to change between now and 1997 (when the change could take place) that the Authority feels unable to offer a positive view so far ahead but offers factors to be considered if it were to be contemplated. The Authority proposes to commission research into this matter. (Radio Authority, 10–11, p. 5).

3. The Association of Independent Radio Companies is even more cautious:

... in questioning the present role of the BBC's popular music-based services (Radios 1 and 2) we are not advocating the privatisation of one or both of them, but we recognise that other respondents to the Green Paper may do so and, therefore, we wish to comment on this.

AIRC has said repeatedly to the Government and to the Radio Authority that the development of Independent Radio – which it strongly supports – must be carefully planned and conducted at a pace which ensures that growth in the number of commercial services does not race ahead of the ability of advertising markets, national and local, to support them.

The 'quantum leap' theory – that if UK commercial radio's share of all listening suddenly expanded from the current 38% (RAJAR, January 1993) to around 70%, there would be a huge and immediate increase in radio spending – is not supported by AIRC. We believe there is clear evidence to support our contention that additional services, bringing much greater airtime availability, do not guarantee a greater share of advertising spending. The London market is a case in point.

AIRC believes that the UK commercial radio sector is capable of further growth, but it must be steady growth, seeking all the time to consolidate on the gains made in the numbers of services and listeners and translating those gains into real revenue growth before introducing new services. (Association of Independent Radio Companies, p. 2)

4. In contrast to the cautious privatisers a number of respondents specifically point to the public service aspects of the BBC's more popular national radio services:

There has been some debate over whether the BBC should continue to run so many national radio channels and a suggestion that either Radio 1 or Radio 2 should go or be incorporated into another station. Age Concern would be opposed to either of these moves. Along with many other voluntary agencies we welcome the news and social action opportunities given by the speech-based content of Radio 1, for this enables us to reach a large, young audience which we might not otherwise reach. Radio 2, with an excellent range of programmes such as the Jimmy Young programme and Gloria Hunniford, gives us access to a wide range of people in early to middle age as well as those who are already retired. Radio 4's *File on Four*, *Woman's Hour* and *You and Yours*, (to name but a few) inform and educate a wide range of listeners of every age. The high speech based content of these BBC channels give us opportunities that commercial radio cannot offer with its primary concentration on music. (Age Concern, pp. 3–4)

Broadcasting Support Services is an independent registered charity founded by the BBC in 1975 ... as an organisation dedicated to running helplines and providing follow up services for viewers and listeners. ...

Some of our most effective services accompany Radio One and more recently Radio Two programmes. These networks reach mass audiences and are received as highly credible. They do not preach nor are they perceived as vehicles for advertisers. Hence individuals, who do not respond to any other information or education on the matter in question, will respond to educational and social welfare initiatives carried by these networks. The initiative may be drugs or AIDS or teenage pregnancy. This appeal factor is recognised by the UK government in the funding provided for our follow up services on these networks. The introduction of advertising on these networks would damage this important function. (Broadcasting Support Services, pp. 1–2)

All-News Radio

5. Responses to the Green Paper were submitted before the BBC's announcement, in October 1993, of its decision to locate its news and sport channel on the Radio 5 medium wave frequency. Nevertheless we record the views of several organisations. Scarcely any respondents expressed positive enthusiasm for an all-news radio channel and a significant number were very specifically critical of it:

> ... this new news service will, it is reported, cost £9–10m to set up; on the evidence of letters to the Campaign, the public demand for this is so minuscule as to throw serious doubts on the wisdom of spending such a vast sum of money on an untried (in the UK) broadcasting 'formula'.
>
> In letters to the Campaign, many listeners write that, in their opinion, there is 'enough news' (or, even, 'too much news') already. ...
>
> It is now apparent that the much-quoted BBC audience research, on which the BBC based its assertion that 'most people' want 'continuous news', never asked its respondents (1,300 adults) if they would like this new news service *instead* of Radio 4 long wave. In the months October 1992–March 1993, the question was everywhere asked repeatedly: what was the size, age and socioeconomic group of the sample, and what questions were asked. Answer came there none, from the BBC policy-makers. Finally, the answer did come – a revelation – as a result of one man's (Chris Dunkley, of the *Financial Times*) initiative, on the 'Feedback' programme of 12 and 14 March 1993. The BBC has yet to apologise publicly for misleading everyone – MPs and licence-payers – by publishing 'sophisticated' results purporting to be derived from sophisticated research. This is, in some places, construed as a serious breach of trust; the word that comes to mind is 'duplicity'. (Campaign to Save Radio 4 Long Wave (UK), 3.2, pp. 7–8)

The BBC intention to go ahead with an all-news radio channel is mistaken. Contrary to some British assertions, the now long-established American all-news stations have not been a huge success; more successful have been all-talk stations which often focus heavily on sport – rather like the BBC's current Radio Five. The BBC mistake has been to leave Radio Four largely unchanged (except for the revolutionary move of *Woman's Hour* from afternoon to morning). Radio Four's weekly audience includes a massive four million members of the AB middle and upper-middle class; nearly half of the Radio Four audience is aged over 55. With support from selected newspapers and MPs, the Radio Four audience is one of the most effective pressure groups in Britain.

The BBC already offers an extremely varied selection of predominantly talk-radio offerings – Radio Four and its regional versions, the BBC local stations, and of course Radio Five whose muddled output attracts, according to RAJAR, just 1.3% of UK radio listening. Radio Six would be one talk channel too far. The BBC needs to rethink its entire radio speech output, which means grasping the nettle of Radio Four. (City University, Communications Policy Research Unit, 8, p. 14)

Radio 5

6. It is also worth noting, in the light of the BBC's subsequent decision, that a number of responses which were broadly supportive of the BBC maintaining a full range of services included reservations about the current direction of Radio 5:

> In principle, the BBC should continue to retain its current programme services. It should, however, reconsider the role of Radio 5, which has not proved to be a success. (Church of England Communications Committee, 14, p. 3)

> The University believes that the current number of the BBC's national network services should be retained, certainly for television, and probably also for radio. Its view is that it would be difficult for it to perform an adequate public service broadcasting role with a reduced number, particularly as regards television, and certainly to perform the role the BBC sees for itself in 'Extending Choice'. It is concerned at the suggestion in the Green Paper that the BBC 'could have a service entirely for education and training programmes' and does not support this approach. The University is already concerned about the dangers of creating an educational 'ghetto' arising from the establishment of Radio 5, and strongly believes that the wider value of educational programming can only be fully achieved if it is incorporated in a network with a wider scope and appeal. It is only by including education in a broadly based network that the benefits of accessibility to a wide audience ... can be achieved. Only in this way can an audience be reached, which might not be attracted to an 'education' channel. (Open University, 4, p. 2)

7. However, only one respondent presented a radical proposal for how Radio 5 might be changed:

Radio Five should be redefined for a young audience, and, as a long term development proposal, give that audience a focus with an alternative cultural view with a base outside London. Since Manchester is already home to network TV youth programming, we would favour the relocation of Radio Five to Manchester. (Mersey Television, 18.v, p. 11)

Local Radio

8. A number of responses questioned the utility of at least some of the BBC's local radio:

> If the English radio and TV regions are arguably too large, much of BBC local radio, intended to serve smaller but genuine communities, has failed to develop a distinctive personality or *raison d'être*. BBC local radio provides, perhaps, a prime example of the result of chasing audiences in competition with commercial rivals. A local radio station geared specifically to providing a public service in line with the BBC's 'Extending Choice' objectives would presumably be unprofitable in commercial terms and unviable in terms of audiences.
>
> We believe, therefore, that the BBC should give serious consideration to its future involvement in local radio, and in those cases where a local service fails to meet the BBC's own criterion of providing an original contribution compared with what is otherwise available, it should be withdrawn. A judicious pruning of the BBC local radio network might provide a pool of wavelengths that could be put to better use. (Society of Authors, 5.8–5.9, p. 4)

BBC local radio enjoys an overall market share of 9.5% of which about two thirds do not listen to ILR as well. Its listenership, although small, is extremely loyal, as anyone in the Home Office would testify who survived the deluge of mail which followed even the suggestion in 1978 that the BBC might cut down its local radio operation! On the other hand, it is expensive and the BBC, unless it is to be given a blank cheque, may have to make some cuts.

The output of BBC local radio could be safeguarded by a promise of performance, requiring any independent operator to maintain the same proportion of speech as at present. If BBC local radio is producing a large audience, such a service could be viable in the private sector; if it is not delivering a large audience, it is arguably a waste of a frequency; and if the audiences were really low, there is certainly no case for the service being continued. (Radio Clyde Holdings, 2.2, pp. 11–12)

9. The Association of Independent Radio Companies, however, drew a rather different conclusion from the relatively expensive but low audience nature of local speech-based radio:

> On page 30 of 'Extending Choice' the BBC underlines its commitment to 'delivering high quality local and regional journalism' in radio and AIRC totally supports this. This is not a viable option for local and regional commercial services, because quality speech radio is expensive and does not command large audiences. But there is a real public service need here and in this respect BBC local radio can be most effectively complementary to Independent Radio's ever-widening range of music-based services. (Association of Independent Radio Companies, 6, p. 4)

10. A defence of a mixed diet on BBC local radio came from the National Union of Journalists:

> The NUJ is of the firm belief that local radio is an integral part of the BBC's structure and must remain so. BBC local radio stations provide a service to their respective listening public that no other broadcaster provides or attempts to provide. Its news and information services are vital to the communities they serve as are the many community ventures BBC local radio participates in. This is all the more so given the poverty of news and speech content in most ILR stations. The NUJ welcomes the BBC's commitment to news and current affairs in local radio and its transition to a predominantly speech based network but the same qualification applies, namely that the mix of programmes should be balanced. Evidence suggests that the audience are happier with a mix of speech/music and a retreat into a hundred per cent 'speech based ghetto' would cause BBC local radio to lose more listeners rather than gain more. (National Union of Journalists, p. 5)

11. In one area of the country – London – there is a predominantly speech-based commercial local radio. This prompted the following conclusions from the Radio Authority:

> The [Radio] Authority welcomes the BBC plan to move its local radio services to a mainly speech-based format, using the BBC's strong news-gathering resources. In many parts of the country ILR would be unlikely to provide services of that character, so that their withdrawal by the BBC would reduce the range of service to listeners. However this is not true of London, where ILR has since

1973 (through the present licensee, LBC), offered an almost 100% speech-based service, with high news and information content, which has consistently attracted much higher audiences than the BBC's local radio station. As Independent Radio continues to develop and expand its range of outlets in the years ahead, the position in London is likely to be matched in some other major cities. In the view of the Authority, there is no need for the BBC to continue to use public funds for speech-based local radio stations in those areas where the independent sector is able to meet this audience need. (Radio Authority, 12, p. 6)

BBC Radio Commercialism
12. From commercial radio operators and others there was considerable criticism of BBC radio straying too far into the commercial area and into commercial practices:

The range of BBC radio services should continue to be wide because the range of interests of the public is manifestly wide, but breadth of range should no longer continue to be pursued for its own sake. BBC Radio should target the many strands of programming, some wide in appeal, such as popular drama, light entertainment, sport and local and regional speech-based programming, and some of specialist interest, such as coverage of the arts and politics, which cannot form the basis of viable commercial services.
However, in chapter 4 [of *Extending Choice*] it is asserted: 'The BBC is therefore well used to adapting its radio services in order to respond to a changing market.'
How well Independent Radio knows this! ... Radio 3 re-positioning itself for the launch of Classic FM, BBC local stations apeing the music-based style of local commercial stations, Radio 1 tiptoeing through the Licence and Agreement in order to offer nakedly 'commercial' tie-ups with sponsors.
Our point is that BBC Radio has to take its place in the total pattern of radio in the UK and this can only be achieved by effective external regulation. It cannot go on marauding about preempting the regulated independent sector as and when it chooses. (Association of Independent Radio Companies, 2, pp. 1–2)

The [Radio] Authority views with concern the current level of BBC sponsorship activity, and considers that sponsorship should be discarded as a method of funding for the BBC. Sponsorship is, in effect, a form of advertising expenditure; in any commercial enterprise there is a limited amount of money available for either advertising or sponsorship, and if it were to be substantially switched into sponsorship for BBC programmes the independent sector would be deprived accordingly. It is accepted that BBC Enterprises should seek to earn revenue from the sale of programmes overseas, the sale of tapes and CDs of earlier programmes and the sale of goods bearing its logo but it is, in the Authority's view, wrong for the BBC to seek sponsorship money in order to make or support programmes. (Radio Authority, 9, pp. 4–5)

Regulation of Radio

13. Both the Radio Authority and the AIRC argued the case for a single regulator embracing both BBC radio and Independent radio:

As part of the system of licensing and control, the Radio Authority has found it necessary to develop the concept of 'Promises of Performance'. These prescribe in some detail the programme format licensed, which cannot be departed from without Radio Authority approval; this is not lightly given, because to do so would undermine the basis of the original competitive process and the 'consumer guarantee' of enhanced listener choice which the Promise of Performance constitutes.

In contrast, the BBC has virtually total freedom to change programme formats. A conspicuous example is the current plan to change Radio 4, on one of its frequencies, to an all-news service. If the BBC were the only broadcaster, this flexibility might have more advantages than drawbacks for listeners. But in a competitive environment, it is unfair if one sector enjoys freedom – including freedom to pre-empt the other – which for regulatory reasons must be denied to the other sector. The Radio Authority would like to see the equivalent of Promises of Performance applied to the BBC, either through its post-1996 legislative environment or – better – through establishing a single regulatory regime – see below.

Following on the idea of Promises of Performance for all radio services, the Radio Authority sees merit in the concept of a single regulatory body for all sound broadcasting in the UK. This would make it possible for the distribution of frequencies to be handled by an authority independent of frequency users; for a common Promise of Performance regime to be developed across the board; and for listener complaints – an aspect of regulation to which the Authority attaches importance and pays close attention – to be dealt with on a common and independent footing.

46

If a single regulatory body were established, the BBC Governors would adopt a role more akin to that of non-executive directors in a company.

The Radio Authority recognises that a single regulatory body riding the two horses of publicly-funded and commercially-funded services would have a complex task. But the idea of a single body has enough attraction to make it worth the effort to devise a scheme. (Radio Authority, 14–18, pp. 6–7)

AIRC urges the Government – as it has done since 1986 when it made its first recommendations on radio reform – to adopt a single regulator for *all* radio.

Chapter 8 of 'Extending Choice' argues for BBC programming to be properly regulated, but we do not believe this can be achieved by any body which is part of the BBC. A regulatory body which 'should hold the BBC's management to account, ensuring that it consistently meets its Charter obligations' must be independent of the BBC, as the Radio Authority is of the Independent Radio licensees. And, as we have stated repeatedly, BBC Radio cannot be regulated independently of the regulation of the rest of radio, otherwise we will continue to have the wasteful use of spectrum and duplication of programme services which we have already commented on at length.

The case stated by the BBC against having a single regulator for all radio is not, in our submission, a convincing one. Far from facing a dilemma, as is suggested, in having 'an obligation to support' services on the BBC which were directly competitive with those provided very adequately by the commercial sector, the regulator would have a duty to ensure – as the Radio Authority does now within Independent Radio – that they are *not* the same! (Association of Independent Radio Companies, 18, p. 8)

Independent Production and Producer Choice

Introduction
1. Traditionally virtually all BBC television programmes have been produced in-house using in-house facilities. In recent years that has changed radically in two ways. First the BBC has been subject to a 25 per cent quota of independent production for television programmes, recommended by the Government in 1987 and made statutory by the 1990 Broadcasting Act. Second the Corporation has adopted as a central part of its strategy the policy of Producer Choice. Coming into operation in April 1993 Producer Choice establishes not only an internal market for facilities for BBC-produced programmes, but also a market which is open to outside competition. Both independent production and Producer Choice are the subjects of a considerable number of expressions of concern by respondents to the Green Paper.

Maintaining an In-house Production Base
2. Very few responses criticised the independent production quota. One of these was the Campaign for Press and Broadcasting Freedom:

> The Producer Choice system should be abolished. The logic of Producer Choice is to erode the pool of established skills within the BBC. This will mean that, as a commissioning outfit, the BBC will reach a stage where it is no longer able to sustain a culture of innovation and challenging, quality programming. In addition, we believe that it is illogical, unreasonable and inconsistent to expect the BBC to provide 'programme services ... that are or might be at risk in a purely commercial market' through an internal commissioning system that is solely determined by the market.
>
> In terms of access to independent programme makers, it is our view that the current system of legislation (the 25% Rule) has failed to significantly stimulate diversity, and has promoted fragmentation, casualisation and low wages. The system also has

serious implications for equal opportunities within the broadcasting industry, making monitoring of appointment and working practices much more difficult.

There should be no fixed quota for independent production for the BBC. Independent production should not become the predominant system of production in the BBC, nor should it exist and be sustained at the expense of the centres of excellence that already operate inside the BBC. (Campaign for Press and Broadcasting Freedom, 2.2–2.4, pp. 2–3)

3. However, a larger number of respondents went out of their way to emphasise the need for the Corporation to maintain an adequate level of in-house production:

Just as the BBC is the keystone of broadcasting, it should be the keystone of production. Commissioning programmes from independent producers should be an added way of meeting viewers' and listeners' demands, not an obstacle to it. The BBC never had a monopoly over the best ideas, talent and creativity and it is increasingly becoming an enabler of production as well as a producer itself. But the way the BBC can foster and best take advantage of the independent sector is by continuing to be a major producer in its own right. It needs the critical mass of production resources and expertise to prevent the erosion of innovating energy which a fully commercial system would tend to entail: independent producers need a strong BBC as much as the BBC needs them. (British Screen Advisory Council, p. 2)

Channel 4 believes that not only should the BBC continue to broadcast a wide range of programmes, it must continue to make them, too. Channel 4 is the first to recognise the value of independent production. Our own operation as a publisher-broadcaster has been an important addition to the fabric of the British broadcasting industry. Whatever our reservations about the imposition of statutory quotas in a market place, we are delighted that both the BBC and ITV have discovered the benefits of commissioning at least 25% of output from independent producers. This will strengthen the sector. But there must always be a role for the producer-broadcaster in British broadcasting. Such organisations are necessary to maintain the base of production skills, to ensure adequate training and to support an indigenous production industry. The current mixture of producer-broadcasters and independents has encouraged an expanding and flourishing television production industry. It is our view that without strong producer-broadcasters the industry risks becoming too casualised. This happened in the film industry with devastating effect on British production. It reduced audience choice and the British film industry has become almost entirely dependent on US investment and product. (Channel Four, 3, p. 2)

The BBC's main function should continue to be the provision of a programme service, the majority of which should be produced in-house. While we welcome the quota for independent productions, continuity of experience and expertise which is vital to the industry as a whole can only be sustained if most of the programmes are produced by BBC staff. After all, many independents received their initial training at the BBC, and the BBC should continue to make training a major priority. Consideration should, however, be given to increasing the number of services which could be contracted out. Some research, for example, has in the past been jointly funded with other bodies. The development of Producer Choice will allow the freedom not to use BBC facilities. The potential spare capacity this could create in technical services should be marketed to independents commissioned to make programmes for the BBC, so that the commercial potential of the BBC can be maximised. Care will need to be taken, however, that the BBC as an organisation does not die the death of a thousand cuts. (Church of England Communications Committee, 17, p. 4)

Producer Choice
4. Underlying these worries about maintaining an in-house production base seems to be a concern about the policy of Producer Choice. This is put most forcefully by BECTU:

The broadcasting industry believes that the BBC has more to fear from its current management than from the review initiated by the green paper. BECTU subscribes to this view.
The BBC has introduced a policy called Producer Choice. It claims that this policy will make it more efficient and cost effective. The government appears to have accepted the BBC's claims for this policy; yet no detailed analysis has taken place.
Producer Choice is intended to transform the corporation's programme making activities by requiring each BBC department to perform as a business unit. Preparations for the introduction of these business units on 1 April 1993 have led to a 10% reduction in the BBC's United Kingdom resource base. In simple terms this

means that adding the 10% reduction in the size of the resource base to the 25% of BBC programmes made by independent producers, at least 35% of BBC programme making activities now takes place in the private sector. It is the clear intention of Producer Choice to move even more activities into the private sector.

The business units created by the new policy will operate in a totally artificial market place. They will have no control over their overhead costs, such as rent, heating and lighting. They will be required to follow corporate BBC policies on safety and equal opportunities which will add further costs while competing with small privately owned facility companies who will be under no such requirement. The BBC business units will be able to bid only for BBC work; their competitors will be free to bid for work across the entire broadcasting industry. BBC business units will be required to equip themselves to service a public service broadcasting organisation, whilst their competitors will operate on a purely commercial basis. If BBC business units fail to break even, they will face closure and their work will be moved to the private sector.

BECTU rejects the BBC's assertions on Producer Choice. It believes that it is damaging to the BBC as an organisation, damaging to the BBC as a broadcaster, damaging to the BBC as an employer and damaging to the BBC's record as one of the world's most cost-effective broadcasters.

BECTU believes that the cost of producing programmes will increase dramatically in real terms as a direct result of Producer Choice. The real truth is that no one at the BBC can foretell what its long term consequences will be. It has been introduced as a political expedient; an attempt to deflect government criticisms of the BBC during the debate on the charter. BECTU agrees that the BBC must be seen to offer value for money but we believe that the BBC has clearly demonstrated this as the United Kingdom's main producer of radio and television programmes.

The policy of Producer Choice will change the BBC from a major programme maker into a publisher/contractor of programmes. BECTU believes that there has been a high degree of viewer and listener satisfaction with the BBC services, and that those seeking radically to change the BBC, whether they are the existing BBC management or others, must be made to justify their position before that change is made.

Senior management at the BBC do not share the union's view of this policy. At senior level, the director general and board of governors believe that Producer Choice will benefit the BBC, but no other issue has divided management and staff as Producer Choice has.

If senior management are wrong in their assessment of Producer Choice, the damage inflicted on broadcasting in the United Kingdom will be irreversible.

If the government wants a public debate on the future of the BBC it should demand that the BBC defer the introduction of Producer Choice until that debate has been concluded and the government has published its plans. (BECTU, 1, pp. 1–3)

5. In more general terms these criticisms are shared by a wider range of respondents:

The comprehensive restructuring programme centred upon *Producer Choice* – the introduction of an 'internal market' system similar to those imposed upon the national health and education services, which many professionals in the industry believe will undermine its production capacity and increase production costs in the long run – has pre-empted genuine public debate about alternative strategies for its future, and was based entirely upon an internal review of how it should plan for the future. (Labour Party, 1.14a, p. 5)

6. One particular worry about Producer Choice voiced in a number of responses is its threat to production facilities outside London:

The introduction of Producer Choice may have profound and possibly irreversible implications for production outside London, and consequently for culture, education and the arts outside London. (Mersey Television, p. 17)

There is a concern that Producer Choice reduces the options for the BBC in pursuing a coherent training policy. Effective training is only possible where a production centre exists and we would strongly argue that, in order to continue to develop and train talent in Scotland to provide a culturally relevant view of the country on the network, it is necessary to maintain a production base here in Scotland for both radio and television. (Scottish Arts Council, 4.4, p. 5)

7. Intriguingly, one London-based respondent identified some of the same effects of Producer Choice but saw them in a more positive light:

The BBC commitment to creating an internal market for production services based on 'producer choice' is likely to lead to a change in the balance of employment between BBC staff and independents. As London has the UK's greatest concentration of independent producers, in both television and radio, this is likely to have considerable benefit for them and for the further development of a critical mass of skills-based broadcasting sectors, with consequent benefits for employment in the London area. (London Arts Board, 4.1, p. 2)

8. Equally intriguingly one of the few positive defences of Producer Choice came from outside London:

TAC [Welsh Independent Producers] supports the current implementation of producer choice which allows the BBC producer to select the best facilities for the job; whether they be in-house or an external supplier. The same principle should be extended to the BBC scheduler and commissioner to allow him/her to select the best producer for the job; whether they be in-house or an independent production company.

Transparency, fair-dealing and fair competition need also to be established in the BBC's dealings with different independents. This is not the case at present. (TAC – The Association of Welsh Independent Producers, 5.3–5.4, p. 8)

Commissioning
9. This concern expressed by TAC about commissioning procedures for independent production is amplified by the British independent producers' trade association:

When independent production was forced upon the Corporation as an additional editorial strategy and an unwelcome economic discipline, the BBC failed to properly integrate independent production into the corporate machinery.

PACT believes this failure continues to have important effects upon the editorial standards of BBC programme output as well as providing a trading environment that is markedly different from some other broadcasters whose conduct in this respect is defined by the Office of Fair Trading.

PACT believes this structural weakness – which at first sight appears to present a simple problem of commercial disadvantage for certain parties – has in fact consistently precluded the widest choice of programme ideas from being considered by commissioning staff at the BBC. Inevitably it is the viewing public which has been the loser.

The BBC urgently needs to introduce a commissioning system that enables the selection of the best programme ideas regardless of their origin. The assessment of independent producers' programme proposals should not therefore be undertaken by in-house programme production departments who are in fact competing with independents to supply programmes to BBC 1 and BBC 2.

PACT believes that in the short term, commissioning editors should be appointed to each programme group to finalise the selection of projects from which the channel controllers choose the schedules of BBC 1 and BBC 2. In the longer term, the channel controllers should be replaced by a Director of the Television Service to oversee a Channel 4 type commissioning editor system. Business Affairs departments should exist for each programme area dealing with a supplier base that includes in-house production but extends out into the independent sector and the facilities market.

All network programme budgets should be centralised within each programme area. So whilst the BBC should be geographically devolved for the in-house production, editorial and 'compliance' aspects of network programmes (including output from Scotland, Wales, Northern Ireland and all the English Regions), the 'buying' policy and specific commissioning decisions relating to each programme area should be made centrally.

PACT sees no reason why the Office of Fair Trading should not monitor the BBC's programme commissioning process as it does the Corporation's adherence to the 25% independent production quota. Indeed the precedent already exists in the OFT's involvement with the ITV commissioning system. (PACT, 5, pp. 10–11)

Public Service Broadcasting

Introduction

1. As we have seen, most respondents seemed happy about the BBC continuing to deliver the range of services and programming the Corporation currently provides. However, a significant number were uneasy about the way the BBC philosophically underpinned its strategy, particularly *Extending Choice*'s stated goals of 'performing a set of clearly defined roles that best complement the enlarged commercial sector', and 'eschew[ing] programming of a type and quality that can be found in abundance elsewhere'.

Complementary Programming

2. The ITC found a deep ambiguity in the BBC's formulations:

> Few would dispute that publicly funded television should be expected to provide specific types of material in the public interest, such as informative and educational programmes, high quality drama and coverage of national events. A question posed by the Green Paper (for example in section 4.5) is whether the BBC should also broadcast programmes of a lighter type where the 'public interest' content is more questionable, bearing in mind that an increasing choice of such programmes is likely to be available as the commercial sector develops further.
>
> The BBC's own response to this question is ambiguous. On the one hand its own document, *Extending Choice*, says that the BBC 'should withdraw from programme areas or types in which it is no longer able or needed to make an original contribution' and 'eschew programming of a type and quality that can be found in abundance elsewhere' (page 32). On the other hand it is difficult to identify from its own statement what significant changes there might be under this plan. There is evidently no intention to withdraw from any specific areas of entertainment for example, even

though these are often already well supplied from commercial sources. At best the BBC's position appears to be a commitment to withdraw from unsuccessful light entertainment formats. There is no indication that the BBC would drop soap operas such as *EastEnders*, which it produces itself, or *Neighbours*, which it buys from Australia.

We would not be as fearful as the BBC that the confining of 'public service' values in broadcasting to a narrow base of publicly funded television, which, as the BBC correctly say, is a tendency in the USA, Australia and elsewhere (pages 14–15 of *Extending Choice*), is a serious prospect in the UK. Comparisons with other countries are often misleading. Their broadcasting systems have developed in different ways to ours. The funding of public television from a mixture of public and commercial sources, which occurs in many other countries in Europe and elsewhere, is often to blame in putting the public broadcaster under serious pressure as the audience share taken by public television continues to fall.

The ITC believes that the BBC should continue as a major producer and supplier of original programming to UK viewers, so that it can continue to provide a wide range of programmes. The present competition between the BBC and commercial channels – not just for audiences but also for professional recognition – across all types of programming, including regional programmes, is crucial to the maintenance of standards in UK broadcasting generally. A balance between regulated commercial channels and wide-ranging publicly funded channels is greatly to the benefit of viewers. Each side is forced as a result to be more sensitive to audience needs, and there is an incentive to maintain levels of UK-produced programming which viewers value most. (ITC, 18–21, pp. 5–6)

3. Others were straightforwardly critical of the whole 'complementary' approach:

The BBC must continue to be the keystone of British broadcasting. In practice this means setting the standards, in terms of range and quality, for other broadcasters to emulate. Rather than the willingness of the private sector to provide a particular type of programme or service meaning that the BBC's involvement is unnecessary, that willingness makes the BBC's involvement all the more necessary. This is for three reasons:

- in its standards-setting role, the BBC must be in the forefront of maintaining and enhancing the quality of output;

- by helping viewers' and listeners' demands to be met, by ensuring that the public continues to have high watching and listening expectations, and by contributing to the enhancement of the quality of radio and television services, the BBC will be stimulating the UK's programme-making resources and, with them, the development and growth of new radio and television markets;
- where there is demonstrable public demand for types of programme, the BBC should also be helping to satisfy that demand.

In both television and radio, the BBC should be active across the entire range of programming, from the very popular to the esoteric. Its special contribution is to ensure that viewers and listeners are exposed to and have access to the whole gamut of broadcasting, and that programmes which extend and enhance viewers' and listeners' understanding and enjoyment are transmitted in peak time; this is not only to make them as accessible as possible but to confer on those programmes the importance and profile they warrant. (BSAC, p. 2)

It is our view that public service broadcasting in the UK should be protected and strengthened. This can be achieved through the realisation that *all* channels have a responsibility to provide a wide range of programming, not just the BBC and Channel 4. For the broadcasting system to operate in a manner which serves the public and not just the market, all broadcast output should have positive public service obligations.

Public service broadcasting should be defined as a set of activities which cover the whole range of potential output and which are not confined to those services which the market cannot or will not provide. (Campaign for Press and Broadcasting Freedom, 1.1–1.2, p. 2)

4. Alongside concerns about 'complementarity' several respondents offered alternative definitions of public service broadcasting based on 'citizenship' and the plurality of cultures which the BBC was to serve:

The primary role of public sector broadcasting is to enhance the benefits of citizenship. Alongside this must be placed a duty to represent the diversity of the United Kingdom's national, regional and ethnic cultures. Complementarity of programming on BBC radio and television with the commercial sector must be maintained and the notion of distinctiveness must be spelt out in terms of positive purposes, not just in negative terms such as 'not commissioning derivative or imitative programming'. We have no illusion that this set of purposes can be achieved without cost: the commitment to innovation and to this articulated public role will require proper levels of funding. The licence fee should be maintained as the BBC's revenue source at a level appropriate for it to discharge the range of agreed policies. (British Film Institute, p. 2)

It is conceivable that the BBC did once represent and communicate a 'British consensus', most obviously perhaps at times of national crisis, celebration or mourning – although it might be difficult to convince the citizens of Glasgow, Belfast or Swansea this was ever the case. In any event few people today would seriously suggest that it is possible for any one broadcaster to exercise a tight grip upon the minds of the UK citizenry. …

Rather than attempt to paper over the cracks of a largely non-existent consensus, the BBC should instead try to amplify the diversity of voices which have emerged out of the fragmentation of society during the past 30 years.

For both factual and entertainment programming the BBC should set out to explore and address the dysfunctions and the dissent and the conflict created by the increasing disparities in age, income, geography, class, gender, religion, taste, 'lifestyle' and politics of the British public.

The BBC should attempt to identify the areas where consensus exists but accept that more often than not it will be exploring issues about which there is no broad measure of agreement.

If the programme mix is right the resulting shows will sometimes achieve high audiences – on other occasions they will not. But in the hands of sensible programme commissioning executives, this recipe need not turn into a diet of boring documentaries, intellectual game shows and agitprop dramas. Nor should it mean an adoption by the BBC of a Channel 4 remit of catering to minority tastes and interests effectively re-defining the BBC only in opposition to the output of other channels.

Informing through entertainment – and indeed just entertaining – are both perfectly acceptable strategies and the BBC should also continue to encourage its programme makers to believe that TV is not a medium of private communication and that working for the BBC carries with it both the duty and the opportunity to communicate ideas beyond the initial circle or team which anchor the programme or inspire the writers. In other words the BBC should aim to provide accessible programming – whatever the *genre*.

Perhaps most important of all, the BBC should be allowed to operate without always having to observe the rules of the commercial market place that govern the other Broadcasters' commissioning and scheduling policies. (PACT, 1–2, pp. 2–3)

5. A number of respondents were particularly concerned that the BBC's emphasis on 'complementary' programming could lead it to downplay popular entertainment:

The Green Paper and the various BBC responses both focus heavily on the multiplication of new channels. But the scale of the 'inevitable' impact of new channels on BBC audience share is seriously exaggerated. ...

John Birt has predicted that the BBC audience share in both TV and radio will sink to 30% by the year 2000. This prediction should be withdrawn, because it could indeed become a self-fulfilling prophecy and lead to the BBC's continuing and terminal decline.

There appears to be a Sargasso Sea of around 30% audience share from which no public service broadcasting system returns. The two German public service channels (ARD and ZDF) have quickly lost over half their audience to several new aggressive commercial satellite channels and they appear headed for terminal decline. The Australian and Canadian public systems have already experienced such decline. ...

In *Extending Choice*, its initial reply to the Green Paper, the BBC hedges its bets but hints strongly that it favours going for the high ground of an up-market strategy of 'quality' and 'choice', rather than 'competition'. Any such up-market strategy will be a one-way ticket to the Sargasso Sea.

The BBC is critically dependent on the approval of three groups – the politicians, the press and the public. If its audience share falls below 30%, the BBC is likely to meet the combined animosity of all three of these groups. Increasing numbers of people will protest that they watch few BBC programmes; press and politicians will increasingly echo and trumpet such complaints, and audience research will confirm their truth. The BBC in its history has never been able to resist the combined criticism of most of the press and most of the politicians. In particular this rising chorus of complaint will lead to erosion of the real value of the licence fee. Declining revenue will lead to a decline in programme performance; the cycle of decline will be in full and irreversible operation.

To avoid entering and sinking in this Sargasso Sea, the BBC must maintain 80% of the ITV and C4 audience share. To do this it needs more shows like *Noel's House Party*, not less. It also needs a realistic strategy for maintaining its existing audience lead in areas such as Comedy and Sport, as well as Current Affairs and Documentary.

A substantial BBC audience share is desirable on national interest grounds. The BBC's existing reputation as a world leader in broadcasting in general and in public service broadcasting in particular is inescapably linked to the BBC's large size. (City University, Communications Policy Research Unit, 1, pp. 1–2)

The NUJ believes that popular entertainment must remain at the heart of BBC programmes while the corporation continues to cater for minority interests. There is no evidence that the licence payers wish the corporation to concentrate solely on information, education and minority interests, the so called 'Himalayan policy'. Indeed, were this to happen, it would be difficult to justify the licence fee in the absence of a mass audience. The BBC's traditional mix of programmes is one of its major strengths and the case for this mix continuing to be the basis of its programming is made by the audience reach highlighted in the Green Paper, with in any single week more than 90 per cent of the population watching BBC television and 60 per cent listening to BBC radio.

The NUJ feels that the present strategy adopted by the senior BBC management and made public by the new Director General, not to compete in areas of popular programming covered by rival broadcasters is fundamentally flawed.

In actually planning for a reduction in audience share, the BBC is throwing in the towel before the fight has started. In the NUJ's view the BBC is well able to compete with all comers in the area of popular entertainment and any retreat from this area by the BBC would not only be bad for the corporation but also, because of the absence of competition of the very highest standard, bad for the entire industry.

While obviously welcoming the BBC's commitment to high quality news and current affairs outlined in its document 'Extending Choice', the NUJ believes that it would be a fundamental mistake to see any single type of programme or programme strand in isolation and that any moves away from genuinely popular programming and the consequent loss of audience share would make a news and current affairs operation the size of the BBC's very difficult to sustain. Also there is considerable evidence that audience figures for news and current affairs programmes are heavily influenced by the popularity of the programmes that precede or follow them. (National Union of Journalists, pp. 2–3)

6. And one respondent stressed the relevance of the point to radio:

Public service broadcasting loses its point if it is merely expected to jog away from whatever happens to be the current theme in the commercial sector, and provide infill where required. ... 'They're doing "pop" so we'll do jazz' ... 'They're doing "classics" so we'll do "country"' ... 'They're pushing sport this year, so we'll major on news'. It is vital for publicly owned radio to continue to flourish across the full range of creative and informative programming, untrammelled by editorial constraints other than the pursuit of excellence and the nurturing of talent. (Heritage Broadcasting, p. 1)

Equal Opportunities and Minority Interests
7. One other important strand in contributions on the general nature of public service broadcasting stressed the importance of incorporating within any definition a commitment to equal opportunities and serving the needs of specific groups who might be particularly disadvantaged by solely commercial provision:

Public service broadcasting can and should provide a lead to others on:

- equal opportunity in employment practices
- reflection in the content of programmes of the changing role and status of women, and should include social policy issues (e.g. health, education, reconciling work and family) especially in factual programmes
- a balanced reflection in representation of women (and ethnic minorities) on screen and on radio.

The BBC wishes to extend choice by guaranteeing access for everyone to services that are of unusually high quality.
The EOC would also like to see a commitment to ensuring access to an accurate and informative reflection of one's own life experience.
In similar vein, the commitment to 'supporting and stimulating the development and expression of British culture and entertainment' should include the cultures of ethnic minority groups and of

women and men in different age groups and life situations. (Equal Opportunities Commission, 14, p. 5)

... the BDA [British Deaf Association] believes that any definition of public service broadcasting should continue to enable Deaf people to access a wide range of programmes; it is predicted that commercial broadcasters would give priority to maximising profits and shareholders' returns, overlooking the needs of Sign Language users who would not be regarded as a sufficiently large, influential, and lucrative share of the market. Accordingly, it is believed that any category of programme to subsequently be excluded from public service would probably not be made accessible via the medium of Sign Language to Deaf people. (British Deaf Association, 1.2, p. 4)

A Covenant or Charter

8. Several organisations were eager for the BBC's public service goals and obligations to be clearly spelt out in detail in a covenant or viewers and listeners' charter:

The Labour Party believes that the BBC's management strategies and programme-making policies should be informed by a Covenant setting out its obligations to licence-fee-payers, guidelines on service quality, and the terms of reference under which its employees and contractors can expect to operate. This Covenant would also provide a basis for measurement of the Corporation's achievements.

The promotion and defence of this Covenant should be placed in the hands of a genuinely *independent and representative Board of Trustees*, the size and composition of which should be sufficient to adequately represent the diversity of British society. The Trustees should be the sole regulators of the BBC, reporting annually to Parliament on the extent to which the Corporation has kept its pledge to the public.

The Covenant should feature prominently in the legislation which empowers the BBC to continue broadcasting beyond 1996, and might take the following form:

In all its broadcasting operations the BBC will seek to fulfil the following objectives as a public service:

a. Programme Range
To make a full range of programmes, catering for the whole

spectrum of public tastes and interests, rather than seeking merely to complement what is broadcast elsewhere.

b. Audience Reach

To make programmes of intrinsic interest to particular groups, whether defined by demographics, national or regional identity, or any other reasonable criterion, recognising broadcasting's unique ability to introduce mass audiences to ideas, interests and cultures to which they might not otherwise be exposed.

c. Programme Quality

To aspire to the highest possible standards of programme-making and transmission in all aspects of the broadcasting process, and to nurture standards of excellence among BBC staff and any contractors commissioned to make programmes on the BBC's behalf.

d. Production Base

To maintain and develop comprehensive programme-making facilities and technical expertise in the English regions, in Scotland, Wales and Northern Ireland.

e. Creative Policy

To offer a platform for new ideas, techniques, and talents in every area of programme-making; to encourage originality and foster creativity; to persevere with difficult or challenging material where it is considered by BBC programme-makers to be of intrinsic merit; and to be prepared to take risks in the knowledge that sometimes they will fail.

f. Training

To maintain and develop relevant and comprehensive in-house training facilities and practices in all aspects of the broadcasting process, and where appropriate, to provide training in conjunction with external agencies and broadcasting organisations to further standards of broadcasting excellence.

g. Research and Development

To maintain and develop a commitment to research and development in fields of technical innovation and audience research; and to ensure that appropriate archives of its research and broadcast output are maintained.

h. Cultural Identity

To be the standard-bearer and ambassador of British-based talent and culture, through the creation of original material relevant to the diverse cultural aspirations of communities within the English regions, Scotland, Wales, and Northern Ireland, and through coverage of public events and spectacles which reflect aspects of Britain's heritage.

i. Children's Broadcasting

To develop programming which entertains, stimulates the creativity and curiosity, and meets the cultural and educational needs of children.

j. Educational Broadcasting

To recognise its pivotal role as an educational resource for all age and interest groups, and to work with educational institutions to provide a full range of programmes appropriate to the educational and vocational demands of contemporary society.

k. Cultural Investment

To play an integral and influential role in cultural renewal by promoting achievement in all aspects of the arts and sciences, and investing in traditional and innovative skills and talents.

l. Public Access and Social Action Broadcasting

To encourage public involvement in broadcasting and a sense of social responsibility, by developing new forms of access to the airwaves including 'open door' and social action programming.

m. Public Debate

To further the democratic process by providing information, ideas and opinions which enable citizens to make informed decisions; to represent adequately significant differences in society, and to allow airtime for the expression of diverse perspectives, values and opinions; to pursue an independent and non-partisan approach to coverage of current affairs, including a duty to investigate, question and challenge the policies, statements, decisions and actions of public and political figures and organisations.

n. Accessibility

To maintain and develop an appropriate range of transmission facilities to ensure that all its programmes and services are available to every licence-payer.

o. Accountability

To operate at all times in such a way as to fulfil its obligations to the licence-payer, including the development of appropriate monitoring systems, and regular reports to the Board of Trustees as to its achievements and any impediments which may hamper its provision of services to the public.

p. Staff

To employ sufficient staff to meet its obligations as defined in this Covenant; to negotiate and enter into agreement on terms and conditions of service for staff with the appropriate trade unions; to promote equal opportunities policies and practices and seek to ensure that the diversity of society is adequately represented at all levels within the Corporation.

q. Merchandising

To make available programme-related material to the domestic market at reasonable prices that do not include excessive profit margins.

r. Advertising

To eschew any form of paid-for spot advertising or commercial sponsorship on its domestic broadcasting services; and to prepare, circulate, and regularly update guidelines which minimise the extent of secondary sponsorship through broadcast coverage of sporting or other events.

s. External Contracts

To ensure that in seeking to widen its reach and availability, in Britain or abroad, any contracts, partnerships or alliances with external organisations do not compromise or prejudice its independence or its public service function as set out in this Covenant. (Labour Party, 3.03–3.05, pp. 11–14)

Voice of the Listener and Viewer proposes that a charter for viewers and listeners be established as part of the Citizens' Charter. It proposes that this charter should incorporate the following provisions:

(i) The maintenance, through the Royal Charter, Licence and Agreement, of the BBC's role in setting standards for British broadcasting, requiring the corporation to provide full and diverse broadcasting services, including programmes of a social character, for all parts of the nation and, through the World Service, to audiences overseas.

(ii) The maintenance of the licence fee as the principal source of finance for the BBC.

(iii) The setting of the licence fee and the parliamentary grants-in-aid for the World Service at a level that enables the BBC to provide the required services to the public.

(iv) A guarantee that broadcasting in Britain will remain editorially independent within the law, free from control by the government of the day or by any institutional, political, commercial or sectarian body.

(v) The requirement that the BBC Board of Governors, the ITC and the Radio Authority will always act in the public interest.

(vi) The requirement for all national television channels to provide a comprehensive service of high quality news, current affairs, arts, drama, music, educational, children's and religious programmes, in addition to high quality entertainment.

(vii) The restoration and maintenance of the principle that broadcast coverage of major national events, including an agreed list of sporting fixtures, is accessible to all licence holders.

(viii) The requirement that local radio stations should provide services to the community in terms of local access, news and information.

(ix) The establishment and maintenance of mechanisms to improve accountability in broadcasting by enabling viewers and listeners to contribute positively to decisions about the range and quality of programmes as well as providing redress for complaints.

(x) The requirement that the BBC and regulatory bodies shall commission research into viewers' and listeners' perceptions of programme quality and publish the results. (Voice of the Listener and Viewer, 9.1, pp. 7–8)

Archive

9. Several organisations which themselves hold film or television archives emphasised the importance of the BBC's output being properly archived, and suggested ways in which that output could be properly maintained and accessed:

The Department of National Heritage's consultation document *The Future of the BBC* recommends ... that archives and libraries might be among the functions that could be 'contracted out' in the interests of reducing the size and increasing the efficiency of the BBC.

Both as one of the United Kingdom's two national archives for film and television material and as a major national sound archive, the Imperial War Museum urges that this policy be carefully thought through and, if adopted, that its implementation be carefully supervised. ...

Effective archiving is a costly undertaking, and one that does not fit well into a typical commercial environment. ...

There are several essential considerations that must be borne in mind in planning the future of the BBC's archives, especially if the decision is taken to 'privatise' them.

(i) The organisations that take over the archives must be committed to the goal of long-term preservation, not short-term exploitation, and should be funded to make such a goal realistic. Such funding is not likely to be available from income generated by use of archive material alone.

(ii) Selection procedures, and other aspects of policy determination, must reflect the potential importance of material collected in preparation for a broadcast programme but not actually used.

(iii) The organisations that take over the archives must be committed to the goal of public access to the materials contained in them.

(iv) Archiving policy must take precautions against the premature deletion of material by re-use and the inadvertent rendering of material inaccessible by the retention of records on obsolete standards beyond the availability of machinery suitable to play such records – both examples of problems caused by recent trends in audio-visual technology.

(v) A policy for the future of BBC archives must address the problem of equal treatment – and especially equal access – to archives in all media. (Imperial War Museum, pp. 1–2, 4)

Neither the Green Paper nor *Extending Choice* make any significant mention of archival responsibilities. Given that the Royal Charter of the BBC obliges it to maintain archives and to make certain arrangements to provide access to its output it would seem that the two documents are sadly lacking in this respect. It is particularly crucial to build into any 'new' BBC a strong commitment to preserving their library footage particularly in the face of new technologies and the danger that this presents in the medium and long-term to older formats and supports.

Currently, the only systematic provision in place is through the arrangement concluded with the British Film Institute in 1990 which provides access to BBC broadcast output for those outwith the Corporation.

The BBC should be empowered to enter into arrangements locally with suitable repositories to ensure that the output of the regions and the national regions are adequately preserved as part of our cultural heritage, and that appropriate access be provided. The BBC should join with other national agencies in support of the introduction of a statutory deposit scheme for film and television in the UK, to embrace national and regional concerns and should be enabled to contribute to the cost of maintaining their archival collections either in-house or through designated archives, to an acceptable technical standard. Within Scotland, the appropriate repository for material produced by BBC Scotland should be the SFA [Scottish Film Archive] given that necessary arrangements and resources have been secured. (Scottish Film Council, 7, pp. 8–9)

Effective and comprehensive archiving for future generations is not a profit-making proposition. However, the transfer of this 'heritage' responsibility to the NFTVA [National Film and Television Archive] which would then take on the responsibility for the preservation of BBC TV, could both ensure that any slimming down of the BBC's own operations does not jeopardise the preservation of its output, as well as assisting in any scaling down of service activities which the Corporation may consider. At the same time it could ensure that the part of Britain's television heritage produced by the BBC is preserved and made available in the national interest on the same basis as is now the case for that produced by the commercial channels.

There is an obvious and recent precedent for this. In 1990, following representations by the BFI, the Government ensured that the changes to the structure of commercial television brought about by the Broadcasting Act did not imperil the nation's heritage by including a clause (185) providing for a statutory contribution to a national television archive by holders of commercial television licences.

The NFTVA's status as the national repository for what is surely the most important contemporary record of Britain's life and culture is ... unquestioned. It is in a position to assume responsibility for the preservation of any material which the BBC may no longer feel able to maintain and an added responsibility for the recording and preservation of BBC output on the same basis as the current ITV and Channel 4 operations would be a major step towards completing the picture and creating a comprehensive archival resource of benefit to the nation as a whole. ...

At present the BBC is obliged under the terms of its current Charter (para. 3(1)) 'to establish and maintain libraries and archives containing material relevant to the objects of the Corporation, and to make available to the public such libraries and archives with or without charge'. ...

It is ... important that the Charter's archival obligations on the Corporation be not only retained but strengthened, in order to ensure that the preservation and accessibility of the nation's broadcasting heritage is not endangered by any reduction in the operations of its primary producer. However, as such a reduction seems very likely and would affect libraries and archives along with all BBC services, we suggest that the strengthening of the obligation take the form of a formal requirement to co-operate with the relevant national bodies, such as the NFTVA and the British Library National Sound Archive, which are in a position to preserve and make accessible BBC programme material in the national interest. ...

A suitable re-wording of the archival clause in the current Charter, part of the section headed 'Objects of the Corporation', would be as follows:

> To establish, maintain and make publicly accessible libraries and archives containing and preserving material relevant to the objects of the Corporation, achieving these aims where appropriate by formally agreed co-operation with nationally established archives and libraries or with appropriate local, regional or national regional archives and libraries, and not to dispose of any of the contents of its libraries and archives without first freely offering such material for preservation in the appropriate national, regional or national regional collection, provided always that correct legal provision for protection of copyright and confidentiality is ensured. (British Film Institute, Appendix IV, pp. 1–4)

The Governors

Introduction

1. Judging from both the formal responses to the Green Paper and more general discussion, one of the most contentious issues in the debate over Charter renewal is likely to be the role of the BBC's Board of Governors.

2. A considerable number of respondents expressed unease with the present position of the Governors. They focus particularly on the confusion of various roles which the Governors appear to combine – engaging in the day-to-day management of the BBC, acting as a trustee for the BBC's public service goals and regulating the Corporation:

> The Governors of the BBC are supposed to be *regulators*, appointed to ensure that the Corporation meets its commitments as expressed in the Charter, Licence and Agreement, and that it remains independent of commercial or political control. It is not their function to become directly involved in the management of the BBC. But in recent years the distinction between the BBC Governors and the BBC Board of Management has become blurred, with the Governors playing an increasingly active and possibly improper role in the internal management of the BBC, undermining public confidence in the independence and integrity of the BBC. (Labour Party, 4.04, p. 15)

> The Authority does not consider the present relationship between the BBC Governors and its Board of Management to be satisfactory. The Governors can be seen as the non-executive directors of a £1.3bn turnover company, their interest focussed on strategy and results, leaving day to day management to the executives. Without in any way impugning the integrity of the Governors, it

70

must be difficult in practice (and certainly in perception) for them to avoid closing ranks with the executives whenever the BBC is challenged. The independent sector, in contrast, is subject to overview by an independent regulatory body which can form an impartial judgement on any alleged misdemeanour and, taking all the factors into account, decide what, if any, sanction to apply. It seems wrong that BBC broadcasters are not subject to such independent oversight. (Radio Authority, 76, p. 23)

The existing Charter places clear duties on the governors of the BBC, but does not inhibit the extent to which they can become involved in the day to day management of the corporation. BECTU believes that the current board of governors have been drawn too closely into the management of the BBC, that their role and that of the board of management have become damagingly confused. If the BBC continues to carry out its current role, it should have a board of governors whose prime responsibility is to protect the public interest. They should remain responsible for the appointment of senior management, but should be required to be more open about their appointments procedure, and ensure that it is consistent with the corporation's equal opportunities policy. The corporation should continue to have a board of management with clear responsibility for the management of the BBC's affairs. (BECTU, 7, pp. 12–13)

A Single Regulator

3. A number of respondents see the solution to this confusion as being to have a single regulator for broadcasting, both BBC and commercial (or more commonly a single regulator for all television and another for all radio).

4. The management consultants Arthur Andersen advance the case for a single broadcasting regulator along the lines of regulators in other industries like gas or water:

The broadcasting market is currently over-regulated. There are too many bodies which have responsibility for regulating different aspects of the same market.

We believe that the whole industry would benefit from the creation of a single regulatory body.

A single regulator will respond to the need for a coherent approach to the regulation and development of the industry as a whole. It will maximise benefits to the industry and the public in areas such as:

- availability and allocation of frequencies: co-ordination to opti-mise the use of a finite resource, ensuring a wide range of ser-vices;
- programming standards: consistent approach to ensure mini-mum requirements of good taste and quality; *and*
- technology: co-ordination to oversee industry standardisation, and ensure a single response to global developments.

[Elsewhere we] detail the duties, powers and structure of regula-tors in other industries. Certain common points emerge. The duties of the regulators include the promotion of competition, the investigation of complaints, the representation of customer inter-ests and control of revenue and capital expenditure. Their powers include the setting of performance standards, pricing, and service remits.

Broadcasting is, of course, different to the privatised utility industries. The need to promote competition is much reduced. A single regulatory body for broadcasting should not be modelled on that for, say, gas or electricity. There would be risks in appointing one individual as Director-General for the broadcasting industry. However, duties and powers similar to those of regulators in pri-vatised industries could be given to a regulator for the broadcasting industry. Its structure might include separate divisions responsible for television, radio, standards of performance, complaints, tech-nology and customer research and liaison. There would be a need for bodies similar to the existing Advisory Councils to represent the views of different groups of consumers. (Arthur Andersen, pp. 17–20)

5. Arthur Andersen then spell out what this might mean for the Board of Governors:

The BBC's management will have greater autonomy under an independent regulator. The BBC should set up a Board of Directors in addition to or in place of the current Board of Management. This would comprise members of executive man-agement and a number of non-executive directors representative of the broader interests in the BBC. The appointment of some of the current Board of Governors as non-executive directors would provide additional corporate governance and ensure continuity in the short term. (Arthur Andersen, p. 23)

6. The possibility of a single regulator for television is explored by the ITC, as one of three options:

The question ... arises whether the regulatory system which now exists in the independent sector – following an extensive period of governmental, parliamentary and public debate – might provide pointers to the future regulation of the BBC. There seem to be three main possibilities. First, within the BBC there could be a clearer and more explicit division of responsibilities between the Governors and the Board of Management with the Governors taking on the regulatory responsibility. Secondly, the Governors could be given responsibility for regulation, but within a two-tier structure where the Governors formed a separate regulatory body, not unlike a holding company, while the BBC as such, with non-executive directors added to its board, took on the operational role. Thirdly, there could be a wholly new single regulatory body which would be responsible for the regulation of all television in the UK. ...

The first option draws upon some of the thinking in section 7.13 of the Green Paper. Within the BBC the Governors would be responsible for regulation. They would be appointed by Ministers but be independent of them and would need to work to a regulatory remit set out in a new Royal Charter or Act of Parliament. But the Governors would not be responsible for the management of the BBC. This would be the responsibility of a board of executive directors appointed by the Governors. However, the Governors would have an important role in relation to those broad programme policy issues which are concerned with priorities, range, mix and, in particular, the satisfaction which viewers and listeners obtained from the services broadcast. In this respect the Governors could be given a specific remit to evaluate the reactions of viewers to the programme services and to promote public debate of the BBC's programme strategy.

The weaknesses of this proposal all stem from the Governors remaining a part of the BBC. As time goes by, and different personalities come and go, it would be difficult to retain the clarity of the initial separate remits for the Governors and the Board of Management. Moreover, the BBC is a large organisation by any standards, and there is merit in having its board consist of non-executive as well as executive directors. If the Governors were to take on this non-executive role then the clarity of separation between regulation and management would be lost. If there were to be non-executive directors as well as Governors within the BBC, then the structure of the Corporation at the most senior levels would be very cumbersome. Perhaps most important however, if the Governors were to be given a special responsibility for monitoring the degree of viewer and listener satisfaction with the programme services, and for ensuring that the public's views were subsequently reflected in programme policy, it would be difficult to demonstrate publicly that this was happening in practice without creating an unhelpful adversarial role within the BBC between the Governors and the Board of Management.

A more workable and more easily understandable model might result from the Governors being established as a body, separate from the BBC, and with its own small support staff. Under this second option ... the Governors would still be appointed by Ministers. The Governors might then appoint a group of non-executive directors to the board of the BBC (but subject to the approval of Ministers) on the basis that the majority of the BBC's directors must always be non-executives. The non-executive directors would in turn be responsible for appointing the executive directors, including the Director General. This is quite like the arrangement which was established under the Broadcasting Act 1990 for the new Channel 4 Corporation.

The licence fee could be paid to the BBC via the Governors, and released to the BBC on the basis of an agreed corporate plan which would be published. The plan would, amongst other things, demonstrate the way in which the Governors' systematic assessment of viewer and listener opinion had been reflected in future policy. As regulators, the Governors would, of course, be responsible for consumer protection regulation. They might also be given responsibility for ensuring that any commercial activities of the BBC were confined to turning broadcasting assets to account, and ensuring that these activities were conducted on a full cost, fair trading basis. There could be a range of sanctions available to the Governors, including a requirement to publish corrections and apologies or not to repeat certain programmes. ... as a last resort, the Governors would be able to replace the Corporation's non-executive directors.

In effect this would create yet another statutory broadcasting body, but this problem could be overcome by defining the Governors' remit in such a way as to embrace the existing responsibilities of both the Broadcasting Standards Council (BSC) and the Broadcasting Complaints Commission (BCC). At the same time, the ITC's role could also be widened so that it took on these responsibilities in relation to the independent sector. ...

The third option, that of a single regulator, can be seen as a logical extension of the second. The relationship between the BBC and the regulator would be the same, and the regulator would also embrace the current functions of the BSC and BCC. In this case, however, the new regulator would also replace the ITC, and provide a single regulator for all UK television services. The approach of a single regulator for publicly and commercially funded services has been adopted in a number of other countries, particularly in North America and Australia, though less so in Europe. The model fits in with growing EC legislation on broadcasting, applying to all types of broadcasters. The main problems with it are the pace and extent of the change that would be involved, together with the size and influence of the regulatory body which would emerge. The core licensing and regulatory activities of the ITC have not long been established, following a period of extensive discussion which inevitably involved a period of uncertainty and instability. There is a case to be made, particularly in the interests of the licensees involved, that this system should be allowed to settle down for a period of years, before further radical change is contemplated. Moreover, the large regulatory body which would emerge from the single regulator option could create problems of its own in terms of accountability and responsiveness, whether to Government, Parliament or the preferences of viewers and listeners. Nonetheless, there is a logic and clarity about the concept which deserves serious consideration. (ITC, 45–51, pp. 12–14)

7. Other respondents, however, are severely critical of the idea of merging the Governors and the ITC into one broadcasting regulator:

In the forthcoming period, Governors need to take on a more clearly defined role. The proposal that the role of the ITC and the Board of Governors of the BBC could be merged in one regulatory authority is not supported by the BFI: there is a widespread belief that this would concentrate too much power in the hands of one small group whose accountability would inevitably be in question. (British Film Institute, p. 9)

It has also been suggested by some interested parties that the BBC Board of Governors be abolished and its regulatory function replaced by the Independent Television Commission or some body evolving from the ITC. PACT believes that such a move would be nothing short of disastrous.
   Apart from the obvious conflicts of interest raised by placing the regulation of both commercial and non-commercial broadcasters in the hands of one body, the existing track record of the ITC

inspires no confidence that the BBC would be in safe hands. The recent treatment by the ITC of the Channel 5 franchise application process and the ITV networking arrangements coupled with the impunity with which several ITV franchise holders are now blatantly disregarding their public service obligations all indicate just how unsafe the BBC would be in the hands of the ITC or any similar body. (PACT, 3, p. 10)

8. A single regulator for radio is advocated by several organisations active in commercial radio:

In the short term the BBC's governing body should be re-established so that it is seen to be quite separate from the day to day activities of the BBC executive. In the longer term the Authority favours a single regulatory body for radio. We do not advocate combining radio and television under a single regulatory body. The two media are quite different. Experience shows that it was right on the disbandment of the IBA to split the regulation of commercial radio from commercial television; it would seem a retrograde step to merge the two media again.

A radio regulatory body would be responsible for planning the use of frequencies; it would appoint all licensees with a view to widening listener choice; if a BBC service was performing unsatisfactorily over a protracted period, and thereby wasting a valuable resource, the regulatory body would expect the BBC Governors to put matters right.

The regulatory body would regulate programming and advertising through Promises of Performance and through codes applicable, where appropriate, to all services. The present Radio Authority already licenses all non-BBC radio services comprising national, local, cable, satellite and restricted (e.g. special event) services, as well as 'additional services' (which may be data or audio services carried on national FM sub-carriers).

By making BBC radio services subject to the same rules as the independent sector consistency would be achieved throughout the industry without reducing the importance of the BBC Governors to direct the strategic aims of the Corporation and to be concerned with its achievements and results. (Radio Authority, 77–80, p. 24)

A radio authority which does not oversee BBC radio will be less able to extend the range of consumer choice. The new services which are introduced by either side might simply replicate those already provided, or anticipate their introduction by the other authority, rather than genuinely extend the range.

A single radio authority could also examine dispassionately whether there was a need for both BBC local radio and an ILR service in the same area. We will not achieve the optimum use of frequencies if the BBC and the independent system are competitors for their use. It is also inappropriate that the BBC is represented on the RPG at managerial level while the independent system is denied representation other than by its regulatory body.

A single regulatory body is required to interpret the rules and to ensure that the promises of performance made by each broadcaster are adhered to. Those promises of performance could clearly reflect the differences in method of distribution and sources of funding. Consequently, quite legitimately, the BBC would be obliged, being uniquely in receipt of the licence fee, to provide more in the way of minority programmes and programmes of British origin than other broadcasters who are required by statute to depend on a source of funding which is linked to their popularity with their target audience. (Radio Clyde Holdings, 1.3, pp. 4–5)

Defining the Governors' Role

9. The probably more widespread response to criticism of the Board of Governors is the belief that if confusions in what it does can be sorted out and its composition improved, then a body responsible simply for just the BBC can act as an effective regulator of the Corporation:

In theory, as public trustees, the BBC Governors are well placed to make the BBC accountable. In order to fulfil this responsibility, they should be distanced from senior management, more representative of the community as a whole, without making the Board too unwieldy and cumbersome, and of truly independent status. (Church of England Communications Committee, 26, p. 6)

The Labour Party would like to see a system of accountability which has credibility with licence-fee-payers, BBC managers and staff, and Parliament.

This would mean replacing the existing Board of Governors with a genuinely independent and representative Board of Trustees to ensure that the BBC meets its statutory obligations, and hears the voices of viewers and listeners. The Trustees should act solely as regulators of the BBC with no management function other than the appointment or dismissal of the Director General and the

Deputy Director General. Their task would be to monitor the plans of the BBC management to meet the obligations laid down in the Covenant, and to measure its achievements. They could invite comment and analysis from bodies representing the interests of viewers and listeners and advise the BBC management about shortcomings, new directions and more effective use of resources. They should defend the BBC from any unwarranted external interference and political pressure. They would report annually to Parliament on the extent to which the Corporation has kept its pledge to the public. (Labour Party, 4.16–4.17, p. 17)

Selecting the Governors

10. There is considerable agreement that selection of the Governors needs to be more open and their composition more representative. But respondents propose a number of different mechanisms to achieve these goals:

> The Board of Governors should be elected. The exact method for election could be arrived at after a full public debate. The method for election should ensure that the range of candidates are representative of wider UK society. (Campaign for Press and Broadcasting Freedom, 4.2, p. 3)

> In relation to Public Appointments in general, it has seldom been the convention to advertise, although there have been some recent exceptions. This [Equal Opportunities] Commission has advised Government that, in our view, the process of public appointment should be akin to normal recruitment, and that open advertising is more likely to result in women candidates being considered than if appointments are made in secret.
> We strongly recommend that appointments to the Board of Governors and other senior appointments, where this is not already the case, are subject to open recruitment procedures. (Equal Opportunities Commission, 9, pp. 4–5)

> A more publicly accountable system of appointing BBC Governors is long overdue, not only for the sake of increased accountability but also as an additional guarantee of independence from the patronage and political interference of the government of the day. We therefore believe that a system of appointment by Select Committee, subject to Parliamentary approval, should now be seriously examined. Furthermore, the composition of the Board of Governors, should in general be required to reflect the society which the BBC serves. (Federation of Entertainment Unions, 12, p. 2)

To improve the status and function of the BBC's regulatory body, a number of options suggest themselves:

(a) Representative organisations could be invited to submit names to the Secretary of State, to ensure as broad a range of potential nominees to the Board of Trustees as possible.
(b) Prior to appointment, nominees could be subject to public examination by Select Committee to ensure an independent, balanced, representative and able Board.
(c) An independent Broadcasting Appointments Commission could be established by Select Committee with power to appoint all, or a significant proportion of, the Trustees.
(d) Places on the Board of Trustees could be guaranteed to representatives of licence-fee-payers in Scotland, Wales, Northern Ireland and the English regions, whether nominated by the relevant Broadcasting Councils, or by election. (Labour Party, 4.22, p. 18)

Public confidence would be improved if there were better and more open efforts made to see that the composition of the Governors reflect the nation in all its aspects. It might be better if the Governors were chosen on the recommendation of the relevant Select Committee. Nominations should be accepted from the public. Candidates for Chairman should be publicly interviewed by the Select Committee. It remains essential that the Governors should not be seen as being 'in the pockets' of any political party. (Media Society, 17, p. 5)

We would like to see the Governors acting more like Trustees of the national interest, representing the licence fee payers as a whole. To this end, we would like to see the national Trustees drawn from regional boards of trustees who themselves will be drawn from a wider cross-section of society, including industry practitioners.

We would also like to see the Trustees make greater use of practitioners' advice from within the industry, as well as having access to independent advice on major matters of public policy. (Mersey Television, 21.iii–iv, p. 12)

Accountability to the Licence Payer

Introduction
1. Discussion around the role of the Governors is only one part of the debate on the accountability of the BBC. Much of the rest of the debate is concerned with how the licence payers can have a more direct impact on the activities of the Corporation.

The Advisory Bodies
2. A starting point for many respondents is the failings of the BBC's current advisory mechanisms, with, however, differences on how fundamental a change is necessary to rectify them:

> BECTU does not believe that the advisory councils and national broadcasting councils have worked effectively. There is clear evidence from public meetings held up and down the country that the general public are unaware of who sits on these bodies, how they are appointed, and what purpose they serve. If these bodies are to be *reformed*, and BECTU believes that they should be, government should have a clear idea what will replace them. This area needs detailed examination before any conclusion is reached. If committees are to be set up to advise the BBC, the method of their appointment, the nature of this remit and their role should be known. The general public should have easy access to them. (BECTU, 7, p. 12)

> The NUJ believes that the BBC should be as accountable as possible to the licence payers. However the present system of local/regional BBC councils is at best ineffective and at worst an expensive farce. Generally the viewing and listening public are unaware of the very existence of these bodies, the membership of which is shrouded in mystery with appointment by patronage. The NUJ's view is that they should be abolished and the BBC should

be fully accountable to its owners, the licence payers, and that this should be achieved by the BBC having a statutory duty to hold regular public meetings in all areas of its activity. (National Union of Journalists, p. 8)

The NFWI [National Federation of Women's Institutes] agrees with the House of Commons Home Affairs Select Committee that in view of the cost and administrative burden of the numerous Advisory Councils, their structure should be reviewed, but the Councils themselves should not disappear. Local listeners' and viewers' panels should be encouraged, and the Advisory Councils should be retained and be as representative as possible of a wide range of community interests. Any changes made to the structure or income of these bodies, however, should not in any way hinder television or radio services' abilities to receive specialist advice when it is required. (National Federation of Women's Institutes, 12.2, p. 5)

3. The Campaign to Save Radio 4 Long Wave cites its own experience:

On the evidence of letters to the Campaign, there appears to be a widespread feeling that BBC policy-makers no longer acknowledge any duty – neither legal, pragmatic nor moral – to licence-payers and tax-payers; and that anything the BBC *says* about being accountable is merely 'lip-service'. One has the impression, too, that the public feels that those who are 'stewards' of public funds should demonstrate a greater sense of the obligations that this stewardship places upon them: to consult the licence-payers *prior* to making radical changes, to reveal how the audience research results have been obtained, to remember whom the BBC is meant to serve, and so on.

The UK Campaign has suggested to the BBC General Advisory Council that the existence of the Council should be better advertised, e.g. in the *Radio Times*, with contact address, so that members of the public could write to this advisory council whose constitution (includes) its 'duty both to keep the BBC in touch with public opinion and to make to the Governors proposals and comments of their own which may be held to reflect informed opinions among the community as a whole'. (Campaign to Save Radio 4 Long Wave (UK), 3.3, p. 8)

Suggestions for Change

4. A number of different advisory mechanisms are proposed by different respondents to try and improve the situation:

> In terms of regional accountability, there should be a system of regionally elected Advisory Boards, with powers to represent the range of interests in their areas. This should include representation of the local workforce within the BBC. The government have stated that this type of administration may lead to 'confused responsibilities' (as stated in the Green Paper), however, they have offered no evidence to support this, and it is our opinion that this is purely an attempt to keep a firm centralised control on the direction of the BBC. If the BBC is to be truly accountable and representative, then the viewing public must be free to play a part in electing who they wish to see advising the BBC. (Campaign for Press and Broadcasting Freedom, 4.4, p. 4)

> The events of the past 10 months or so suggest that there should be a **listeners' forum** (whose existence is widely advertised) which could meet once every six months: meetings at which awkward questions can be asked of the BBC, which the BBC must answer; open meetings which ordinary listeners, the press and other media, can attend as observers; and there should be no reporting restrictions. (Campaign to Save Radio 4 Long Wave (UK), 5.18, p. 10)

Numerous options present themselves for improving opportunities for viewers and listeners to play an active part in the accountability process:

(a) A new Viewers and Listeners Council to represent the interests of all licence-fee-payers could replace some of the existing BBC Councils, the Broadcasting Complaints Commission and the Broadcasting Standards Council. It could monitor BBC and commercial broadcast output; conduct or commission research; make recommendations to the BBC Board of Trustees, the Independent Television Commission and the Radio Authority about codes of conduct; and consider complaints about all forms of broadcast output. It would require the services of staff, and might be funded from a levy upon the BBC, the ITC and the Radio Authority, and/or from the Treasury at a level similar to that currently allocated to the BSC and the BCC.

(b) Autonomous Broadcasting Councils could be established for the English regions, Scotland, Wales and Northern Ireland, representing licence-fee-payers and primarily concerned with programme policy. They could have the right to representation on the Board of Trustees, and the right to make recommendations and challenge BBC management decisions about the allocation of resources where there was evidence that the BBC's obligations to a regional or national area were not being met.

(c) A new system of Advisory Panels, combining specific expertise and representatives of licence-fee-payers, concerned with programme strands or issues of representation, including equal opportunities and the language or subtitling needs of particular audiences, could be established with links to senior managers.

A range of options suggest themselves as a means of empowering the licence-fee-payer:

(a) Greater autonomy could be given to national, regional and local BBC managers to create opportunities for closer involvement with their audiences.

(b) By incorporating newsletters and questionnaires with licence fee renewal documents, and through full use of interactive telecommunications systems as they become more available, the BBC could encourage individual licence payers to respond to and comment upon its performance.

(c) The BBC could develop more viewers' and listeners' groups around strands of programming with their own publications and local meetings to discuss content, quality and value, and to generate ideas for new developments.

(d) The BBC could expand its market research to include quality circles and consultative events targeting specific audience segments, particularly to test the effectiveness of its services for sectional, minority ethnic or other minority interest groups.

(e) More opportunities could be developed for audiences to meet BBC managers, editors, writers, performers, and presenters, to discuss the Corporation's services.

(f) The BBC could encourage audience confidence by nurturing its existing range of access programmes, and investing in a public media education programme to expand communication skills and encourage greater public involvement in broadcasting.

(g) Any audience research carried out by, or for the BBC, on a continuous or an ad hoc basis, should be made publicly available. (Labour Party, 4.23, 4.25, pp. 18–20)

5. Some proposals highlight the need for particular advisory mechanisms to represent particular needs:

> If the BBC is to keep in touch with its audience's views it is essential for advice to be sought and given. RNIB recommends the setting up of an Advisory Council on Disability Issues broadly comparable to the Channel 4 Disability Advisory Group. The Council would be made up of representatives of the main disability groups to advise on such matters as the type of programmes required; how disabled people are represented in the media; how disabled issues are addressed; improving general awareness of the issues; access to information; access to progamme making.
>
> To ensure recognition of individual people's views visually impaired people must be represented in the audience research process, for both television and radio. (Royal National Institute for the Blind, 9.1–9.2, p. 9)

A Broadcasting Consumers Council
6. The most common proposal to improve the accountability of the BBC is for a single consumer body for broadcasting, generally called the Broadcasting Consumers Council. Most advocates of such a body envisage it incorporating the functions of the Broadcasting Standards Council (BSC) and Broadcasting Complaints Commission (BCC). The basic case is put forward by the Voice of the Listener and Viewer and by the Consumers' Association:

> By their nature the BSC and BCC are limited in scope and deal largely with the negative aspects of regulation and consumer protection. No statutory body has the positive role of promoting the interests of the general public.
>
> VLV proposes that a single consumer body be established for British broadcasting, to represent the interests of viewers and listeners. This body would subsume the duties of the BSC and the BCC. It should cover television and radio services, whether originating from the BBC or from commercial broadcasters including satellite and cable services. It should assume a high profile, and its duties should also include:
>
> - supervising the operation of the Viewers and Listeners' Charter;
> - representing the public interest in broadcasting matters;
> - advising the Government on broadcasting policy;
> - developing positive views of quality and standards in broadcasting and encouraging their adoption by broadcasters;

- assuming the main functions of the BSC and BCC;
- handling all types of individual complaints, it being understood that complaints should normally be first addressed to the broadcaster;
- carrying out research associated with these objectives;
- reviewing with the BBC issues such as performance indicators and measurements of quality and other aspects of accountability of the BBC to viewers and listeners; and
- reviewing with the ITC and RA the monitoring achievement of promises of performance.

This body should be governed by a 'Viewers and Listeners' Council', whose membership should represent a broad range of interests. VLV recognises that with a public body, the appointments would need to be made by the Government, but believes that provision should be made for nominations for membership of the Council to come from a range of organisations familiar with the representation of the public interest. It should include regional interests, special interest groups and representatives of the viewing and listening audience.

Government should consider the principle that some of the places on the Council may be open to nominations from outside organisations. VLV believes there would be value in membership of the Council being subject to sanctioning by the House of Commons Select Committee.

The new body would be financed from the combined budgets of the BSC and BCC, currently at least £2 million. Its total annual budget should be sufficient to provide for the necessary research activity without additional public expenditure.

Research commissioned by the BBC, the new council and other statutory bodies should be made publicly available. At present, much current audience research is not available to the public, who ultimately pay for it. It should also be made clear to the public what performance indicators and assessments of audience appreciation are used. (Voice of the Listener and Viewer, 8, p. 7)

... however the advisory councils are reformed, it would be wrong to expect too much of them given their fragmentation, low profile and location within the BBC's own organisational framework. For these reasons, Consumers' Association sees considerable attractions in the idea of a single, fully independent Broadcasting Consumer Council incorporating the existing BSC and BCC and covering the whole spectrum of broadcasting, not just the BBC.

Such a body would be completely independent of the BBC, as it would be of all other broadcasters – but would in turn be well placed to oversee the quality of the BBC's output, and to make detailed, well-researched assessments of the extent to which it and other broadcasters were serving consumer needs as defined above. Its principal functions would be four-fold:

- to respond on behalf of a clearly defined consumer interest to proposed policy changes whether advocated by Government, regulators or broadcasters;
- to initiate proposals for change, on the basis of anticipated future trends or in response to problems not identified elsewhere;
- to research or commission from others the data on which the above reviews and proposals should be based;
- to handle complaints both from individuals and groups, whether as consumers of programmes (in part covered by the BSC) or as the subject of programmes (the remit of the BCC), and to publish the relevant findings.

We envisage that such a body would be able to operate at a cost not exceeding those of the bodies which it would replace but it would have an effectiveness far greater than any of these bodies. (Consumers' Association, pp. 12–13)

7. The Broadcasting Standards Council supports this move to a single broadcasting consumer body into which its functions would be incorporated. It explains why:

The Council is one of two bodies independent of the broadcasting organisations to be charged with dealing with complaints from consumers about programmes or commercials. Its jurisdiction is, very largely, distinct from that of the Broadcasting Complaints Commission; only over some aspects of privacy is there any real overlapping of interests. Both the Commission, established a decade ago, and the Council represent a step away from the complete autonomy of the broadcasting authorities: the BBC, S4C, and the regulators of commercial television and radio, the ITC and the Radio Authority. They reflect an acknowledgement on the part of Parliament that, at least partially, some form of independent recognition should be given to the interests of consumers outside the responsibilities borne directly by the broadcasting authorities themselves.

The Council has established good working relations with the broadcasters at each stage in the handling of complaints and the volume of complaints suggests that it is fulfilling a demand from consumers who value an independent scrutiny by a lay-body of their complaints. The Council's programme of research and its consultations with the public over a number of general and specialised broadcasting issues have also broken new ground on behalf of consumers.

There nevertheless remains some confusion and uncertainty in the minds of the public about the respective roles of the regulatory bodies and of the independent complaints bodies. To eliminate some of the confusion and to give a more effective forum for the consumers of broadcasting, the Council believes that the time has come for the steps already taken in the creation of both the Council and the Commission to be extended, enabling the consumers' voice to be heard in broadcasting issues, not simply over specific complaints, but over a range of current and developing issues.

To give an example of matters broader than programme complaints, the Council has been engaged since 1991 in a series of discussions with representatives of various sections of society over their portrayal in broadcasting. Representatives of different religious faiths, for example, have met Members of the Council, as have representatives of people with disabilities. In particular, arising from its concern with stereotyping, the Council has met a number of women's organisations to debate women's perspectives on a range of issues, including coverage of the 1992 Election. The Council was aware that, in taking these initiatives, it was operating close to the boundaries of its remit, but it felt justified in doing so by the absence of an alternative forum where such debates could take place in a neutral setting. Approaches by consumers to the broadcasters one-by-one weakens the force of their arguments and strengthens that of broadcasters playing on their own ground.

The Council therefore wishes to put forward a proposal for a new body into which its complaints function and that of the BCC would be merged and which would have the wider and more positive responsibility of promoting consumers' interests in broadcasting. In the view of the Council, those interests include broadcasting research of the kind increasingly beyond the broadcasters' resources. There is a need, for example, for a measurement of consumer satisfaction with programmes more flexible than any system currently available. The new body would undertake the publication of research and of other work designed to extend public awareness of broadcasting issues as one means of ensuring a concern with standards. An important aspect of its work could be the monitoring of services to establish the extent to which they were meeting the needs of minorities and providing a genuine extension of choice for the audience. The Council believes that the new body should also be involved in the promotion of media education at secondary and tertiary levels. (Broadcasting Standards Council, 6–10 pp. 2–3)

8. We have already seen above some different views on how such a Broadcasting Consumer Council might be composed. The National Consumer Council, which supports the idea, presents some of the alternatives:

The composition of a Broadcasting Consumer Council will be critical both to its efficacy in representing the spectrum of interests of viewers and listeners, and to its credibility. On the one hand it must not be seen as an elite body, dominated by 'the great and the good', and on the other it will need to be authoritative. There are a number of options.

Classic quango: this is the National Consumer Council model with the additional role of handling complaints. The government would nominate individuals in a personal capacity. The council's statutes would make it clear that the government should have regard for ensuring a proper balance of interests: the elderly, people in rural areas, children, cultural minorities, the church, business, consumer organisations, academics, and so on. The criticism of such bodies is that they are politically biased, a particularly sensitive issue in broadcasting. However, the principal objects of the council's representations will be broadcasters, programme makers and the regulators – the ITC and the BBC governors, rather than government. Furthermore, the National Consumer Council, although criticised for political bias from time to time, has managed to steer a relatively independent course, even when a former Conservative Minister for Consumer Affairs was appointed chairman. ...

Council appointed by outside bodies: certain organisations such as the National Consumer Council, Consumers' Association, the Council for Racial Equality, the Equal Opportunities Commission, and other special interest groups would nominate representatives to the council. This would ensure a degree of political independence. The problem with such an approach is that it could become dominated by specialist interests who would feel bound by a real or imagined mandate. This would make consensus difficult. Inevitably some sections of the population would feel unrepresented by such a system.

Finally it would be possible to devise a combination Council drawing on the best elements of a quango and appointment by outside bodies. Membership could be a combination of government appointments, regional chairmen, and some earmarked seats for particular bodies. This would provide a useful counterbalance to the inevitable problems of apparent political bias within quangos. (National Consumer Council, 5, pp. 9–11)

The Rest of the Broadcasting Environment

Introduction

1. Many respondents noted that the BBC could not be considered in isolation from the rest of the broadcasting environment, and drew attention to the new regime in commercial broadcasting created by the Broadcasting Act of 1990. A number called for changes in the Act.

2. The Campaign for Press and Broadcasting Freedom called for a rethink of the whole basis of the Act:

> It is our view that through legislation contained in the 1990 Broadcasting Act, the government has established pressures within the broadcasting environment which will drive standards down and make it extremely difficult for the BBC to operate as a major public service broadcaster.
>
> The Act removed key obligations to provide public service broadcasting from the Channel 3 companies and Independent Local Radio. These obligations are now confined to the BBC and to Channel 4 – which still need to compete for audience share to ensure their viability as broadcasters. It is our view that this will prove to be a formidable task, and one which the BBC may not succeed in achieving.
>
> The Act prioritises a market-driven system of broadcasting, thus confining the BBC, as a public service broadcaster, to the margins of that system. If the government truly believe that the BBC should continue as a 'major broadcasting organisation', then they need to completely re-examine their approach to broadcasting.
>
> This process should include re-examining: the nature of public service obligations; auctioning of franchises; the readvertisement of contracts; the removal of 'light touch' regulation; the introduc-

tion of measures to limit cross-ownership, promote diversity of ownership and to inject democratic accountability into the whole system. (Campaign for Press and Broadcasting Freedom, 5.1–5.4, p. 4)

Ownership Regulation

3. The most detailed attention to the 1990 Broadcasting Act came from the ITV companies. The ITV Network Centre, the ITV companies trade association, devoted two whole sections of its response to calling for changes in the Act. One section called for the Government to undertake a comprehensive review of broadcasting ownership regulation. This was one element of a lobby which led to the Government's announcement in November 1993 in changes in the legislation to allow ownership of any two Channel 3 licences.

ITV's Proposals

The Government should examine the existing ownership regulations in broadcasting in the light of the major changes that are likely to occur in the industry from the mid-1990s on and in the light of the work of the European Commission in this area. ...

The Government should use the opportunity provided by the BBC Charter Renewal process to include in the legislation revised UK ownership regulations. These should cover ownership of licences for Channels 3 and 5, licences for cable and satellite channels, and cross-media ownership in television, print and radio. ITV believes that the objective should be to prevent undue concentration of ownership both in any particular sector of the media and also across different sectors, while allowing the growth of reasonable-sized companies in all sectors.

The legislation should include provisions to prevent monopolies in the area of encryption technology; or if, as may be the case, it seems that both consumers and producers will benefit from a single encryption system, that this is regulated to allow open access on fair and reasonable terms.

The Government should amend the regulations on the ownership of ITN.

Since the moratorium on takeovers of ITV licensees ends on 31 December this year, we would ask the Government to conduct this examination of existing ownership regulations as swiftly as possible, even if some of any subsequent legislation has to be undertaken after that date.

The Issues

ITV Licences

The 1990 Broadcasting Act reflected the situation as it appeared in 1988–89, when ITV sold around 95% of all TV advertising, when Sky and BSB looked as though they were battling each other into extinction, and when the implications of the emerging digital technologies were perceived by only a tiny handful of far-sighted experts.

The objective of the ownership rules was to retain the federal structure of ITV, partly in the interest of regionalism and partly to prevent the emergence of a few all-powerful commercial companies which could dominate the TV advertising market.

Individual ITV companies are progressively declining in size relative to the scale of their UK competitors for advertising. ...

More important, revenues from subscription and pay-TV services are forecast to overtake ITV's total revenue by 1998. ITV now faces a powerful commercial competitor in BSkyB, a competitor which is a single entity with six channels (as opposed to a federation of 14 separate companies with one channel) and which has few of the programming or commercial restrictions which are applied to ITV. Channel Four, too, now takes considerably more advertising revenue than even the largest of the ITV companies.

ITV as a regional system also inevitably carries the burden of cost of the regional structure that is part of its legislative remit. That structure also gives rise to an unwieldy decision-making mechanism.

In these circumstances the need to restrict ITV companies to owning two licences, of which one can only be a small regional licence, could be damaging to the health of the ITV system (i.e. the five smallest companies account for less than 6% of total revenue). No single ITV company can now occupy a dominant position either as an advertising medium or as a programme supplier. ...

Whatever the ownership base, the 15 regional programme services are safe-guarded by the licences awarded by the ITC in 1991. The issue is not one of regionalism but efficiency and speed of action by ITV in a more competitive market-place. ...

Independent Television News

The ITV licensees are prevented from owning a majority of the shares in ITN. This measure was introduced in the 1990 Act, against the advice of the ITV companies, the ITC and – eventually – ITN itself. It is now almost universally agreed that this section of the Act is irrelevant to the needs of either ITV or ITN.

The new ITN shareholder pattern will doubtless change over the years, and should be allowed to do so. We would ask the Government to amend this section of the Act so that ITN's ownership can be determined by the market.

Cable and Satellite Licences

An ITV company can own 20% of a satellite licence and 100% of a cable licence. However if it uses a satellite link to deliver the cable service to the cable headends it can only own 20% of the cable licence. In short, if an ITV company delivers the tape by motorbike, or by a British Telecom land line, it can own 100% of a cable service but *not* if it delivers it by satellite to the same headends. It is hard to see the logic in this. We would ask the Government to remove the 20% restriction as it applies to these circumstances.

Cross-media Ownership

The 1990 Act created an elaborate web of cross-media restrictions on ownership of newspapers and TV and radio stations in the UK, in many instances limiting the stake which one media organisation could have in another in a different sector to 20%. However the Act did not extend these restrictions to 'non-domestic' satellite licences (i.e. services delivered via the Luxembourg-based Astra satellites) thereby protecting News International's ownership of Sky. ...

With the growing strength of BSkyB clearly this loop-hole should be closed.

Encryption

Encryption of the television signal is necessary for all subscription or pay-per-view services.

At the moment there is one de facto encryption system available in the UK – Videocrypt. This is provided by News DataCom, a wholly-owned subsidiary of News Corporation.

The subscriber management service is provided by BSkyB – which is 50% owned by the News Corporation's subsidiary, News International. There is clearly a competition-policy issue here: it is difficult to see how these News Corporation companies can treat potential rivals to BSkyB fairly when they seek access to these monopoly services.

The new digital techniques will improve the encryption and subscriber management systems needed for subscription and pay-per-view services. They will also offer the opportunity to create a common standard for this aspect of broadcasting.

We believe it will be in the best interests of both viewers and broadcasters if encryption is regulated to ensure that there is guaranteed access to both the encryption and subscriber management services on reasonable commercial terms.

Ownership of Independents
ITV believes that the present rule limiting a broadcaster's investment in independent production companies to 15% without losing the production company's independent status militates against the development and strengthening of production bases – particularly outside London.

ITV has no problem with the 25% independent production quota but in the interest of industry stability, we believe the Government should look again at whether the 15% limit to investment by broadcasters in independent producers is appropriate. (ITV, 3.1–3.2, pp. 10–13)

4. Whereas the ITV companies appeared united on the rest of the ownership issues raised by the ITV Network Centre, they were divided on the question of ownership restrictions on the ITV licence. A majority took the view outlined in the response of Carlton Television:

The prohibition against merging the ownership of large licences has two damaging consequences. First, it prevents the pursuit of economies of scale which Channel 3 must achieve if it is to compete efficiently and effectively, and if it is thereby to maximise the budgets available for original British production. Second, it prevents the development within the UK of television broadcasting companies with the size and experience to compete effectively with existing large European entities within the Single Market.

The regional strengths of the ITV system will not be imperilled by a relaxation of the ownership regulations. The 15 regional licences granted in 1991 are guaranteed by the ITC, which has considerable financial and other sanctions to ensure that they are fully implemented. Rationalisation of ownership in no way undermines regionality: on the contrary, the scope for greater efficiency offers a more secure base for both regional and network programming.

We do not share the view that the problems outlined warrant an extension of the 'moratorium' which gives the ITC discretion to disallow changes of ownership. Such a step would provide no absolute guarantee that Channel 3 licences will not pass into foreign ownership, one of the most frequent arguments made for it. On the contrary, an extension of the moratorium, *without* any change to the large-on-large prohibition, would offer merely the seductive illusion of protection whilst continuing to damage the ITV system by deferring the opportunity for British broadcasters to achieve the competitive strength they will need, both to service Channel 3 effectively and to compete at a European level.

We submit that there are persuasive reasons for the Government now to review the Channel 3 ownership restrictions, and in particular to examine the benefits which will flow from permitting two large licences to be brought into common ownership. (Carlton Television, p. 2)

5. A minority support the position advanced in HTV's response:

It is regrettable that the Broadcasting Act 1990, which set out the framework for independent television broadcasting, did not address in any detail the aims, functions and funding of the BBC. This was a missed opportunity to look at the future of UK broadcasting as a whole. There is now an opportunity to do this in the context of the current Green Paper and the renewal of the BBC Royal Charter in 1996.

Accordingly we would recommend that no further changes be permitted to the current structure of independent broadcasting before that date, in order that the BBC's future can be considered with a level playing field in operation. In particular, we feel that questions of ownership which, in turn, have implications for the stability and long-term strength of the ITV network as a whole, should be postponed. This will mean extending the existing moratorium on hostile takeovers for a further three years beyond 1st January 1994.

Such a policy will have the advantage of allowing the current franchise system to settle down and letting existing ITV franchise holders concentrate on fulfilling their remit to their viewers. It will also enable the Government to take a view on the future operations of the franchise process at the same time as it decides the future aims, structure and funding of the BBC. (HTV, 2.3–2.5, p. 2)

Disparity of Regulation

6. The ITV Network Centre's second set of proposals for change in the 1990 Broadcasting Act concerned the disparity of regulatory requirements between ITV and satellite broadcasters:

Since 1987 there has been a voluntary agreement by ITV companies to commission not less than 25% of programmes from independent producers by 1992 in preparation for this being a legal requirement from January 1993. The BBC is also required by the 1990 Broadcasting Act to commission 25% or more of its programmes from independents.

The ITC requires that ITV must commission 65% of its programming either from independents or in-house producers. The BBC will continue to carry a majority of newly-originated programmes. BSkyB is not required to commission any of its output either from independents or in-house.

Even the EC requirement – that half of the service has to be European in origin – is not applied to the BSkyB service. The National Heritage Ministry has, so far, allowed these services to escape this legal obligation through the loophole of calling themselves, 'Specialist Channels'. It is difficult to see what makes Sky One a specialist channel.

When ITV is being asked to commission 65% of its programming, and at least 51% has to be European programming (a requirement of importance to the health of the British television production industry), the same should apply to the BSkyB channels. These are likely to be profitable and if the Government required 51% European production it would be a major boost to both the television industry and, if applied to the BSkyB film channels, the British film industry also. The French Government apply such requirements to Canal Plus, the French film channel.

ITV believes that the Government should remove these inconsistencies of regulation and frame legislation around the BBC's Charter renewal to do so.

The new legislation should provide a level playing field for all commercial services in terms of regulation. (ITV, 4.1, p. 14)

Equal Opportunities

Introduction

1. A large number of respondents drew attention to the need to incorporate equal opportunities considerations into the debate over the future of the BBC. As we have seen in the section on public service broadcasting, several argued that equal opportunities should be built into the very definition of public service broadcasting. In this section we outline some of the more specific equal opportunities issues raised by respondents.

2. The commitment of the BBC to equal opportunities policies was welcomed by a number of respondents, but several stressed the need to take action to maintain that commitment given the changes taking place in the broadcasting industry:

> The Equal Opportunities Commission is very concerned that increasing 'flexibility' of employment practices in the industry e.g. use of freelance and contracted staff, 24 hour rotas and mobility requirements, can have an adverse effect on female employees (and on working parents generally) who are more likely to work freelance, or on temporary contracts, because of the break to have children.
>
> Mobility requirements and unsocial hours as a norm in certain jobs can effectively exclude women with children, working parents, and others with responsibility for dependants. Other practices may mean women may be forced to give up their jobs or move to a lower grade or less interesting work. The EOC has already had a number of enquiries from such staff potentially or actually affected by the new practices. The EOC's own research (Working Hours of Women and Men in Britain) has shown that women can work all kinds of hours, but that they need time to

rearrange their domestic cover, and are not able to accommodate complete unpredictability in job patterns.

Personnel policies should make it easier for parents and for those with eldercare responsibilities to continue work without loss of security or promotion prospects. Monitoring should take place to ensure that women are not becoming a 'peripheral' group of workers, with mainly men and childless women holding core status jobs.

In those areas where jobs **are** being created, the BBC should consider the use of positive action as a means of breaking down job segregation.

The Commission welcomes the intention behind current BBC policies on the practice of equal opportunities, but recommends careful monitoring of equal opportunity goals so as to ensure they are not undermined by the impact of changing employment practices, staff reductions and personnel policies within the BBC generally. Flexible working arrangements can benefit organizations and their employees, but need to be introduced with adequate safeguards. (Equal Opportunities Commission, 1b, pp. 2–3)

Issues of Disability

3. There were several detailed submissions from organisations representing people with disabilities. Some impression of the range of their concerns can be gathered from the response of the BFI Joint Broadcasting and Disability Group. They recommended:

- That disability issues should be incorporated into mainstream programming and not be treated as a 'minority interest'.
- That consultation structures be set up to inform and advise the BBC, at Corporate, Directorate and Regional levels, on disability issues and representation. Schools programme advisory structures should also have disability representation to ensure the inclusion of appropriate disability images and language in its output.
- That specialist Disability Officers with expertise and responsibility for advising on equal opportunities in employment, training and programme representation be appointed, with a particular need being seen for a Disability Officer (Television).
- That the BBC publish a Corporate Action Plan (such as that developed by the Arts Council of Great Britain) which would state the organisation's policies on disability, its general access and equal opportunities targets (to be achieved by the year 2000) and outlines procedures for monitoring progress towards

those targets at regional level and Directorate level. (BFI Joint Broadcasting and Disability Group, p. 1)

4. The concern that disability should not be ghettoised was amplified by several respondents:

> There is a confusion as to whether 'disability' is 'a minority interest'. Quite apart from any assessment of whether the numbers of disabled people constitute a quantitative minority (one in four families have a disabled person), there is no evidence that disability based programming is unattractive to a majority audience. Disability programming need not be only 'specialist' or 'committed'. It can and should be incorporated into formats which include many other topic areas. This latter approach is so seldom used, that disability inevitably becomes a marginalised strand. Currently 'mainstreaming' disability means the occasional disabled actor in drama, rare disabled presenters in factual programming and a continued concentration in documentaries of personal tragedy stories as opposed to issues. Issues around disability are usually relegated to off-peak hours, rather than to e.g. *Panorama*. Thus, the labelling of disability as 'minority' interest becomes a self-fulfilling prophecy.
>
> The BBC must be a public service broadcaster, but it cannot hope to please all of the public all of the time. However it can and should ensure that its representation of society, in all its many forms, is more evenly spread throughout its programming. (BFI Joint Broadcasting and Disability Group, p. 2)

> Sign Language users can also contribute an alternative perspective on the arts for mainstream hearing society; the BDA has appreciated the recent support given to Deaf drama by the BBC's 'See Hear' team but would wish to see this patronage extended further to bring Deaf culture to a wider viewing public rather than confine it to specialist Deaf programmes. The BDA, for example, would be but one organisation which would value support to enable its Deaf cultural activities to be accessible to hearing people. (British Deaf Association, 3.3, p. 9)

5. The contributions on disability highlight numerous technical and organisational issues which can have a profound effect in limiting access to people with particular disabilities. The Royal National Institute for the Blind gives this example:

One area where sub-titles are used to the detriment of visually impaired people is for the translation of non-English speaking contributors, particularly in current affairs and documentary programmes. It is extremely frustrating for a visually impaired viewer to have been able to follow a programme well only to lose some of the content because of translating by use of sub-titles, rather than by voice-over. RNIB has raised this issue with broadcasters. There appear to be no guidelines, so producers do what they think is most appropriate for the programme without any regard to the visually impaired viewer. This is not acceptable. To provide a voice-over translation would improve the quality of viewing for visually impaired people. (Royal National Institute for the Blind, 4.2, p. 3)

Issues of Race and Culture

6. A number of respondents made reference to the need for the BBC to properly reflect the ethnic and cultural mix of the United Kingdom on screen. One response, from black independent producer, Stella Orakwue, detailed the failure of the Corporation to use black production talent adequately:

... there is a direct link between the shameful lack of usage of black production talent by the BBC and the 'black' content of the programmes we watch on BBC television.

First, production. Between the period July 1991 and June 1992, ... the Producers' Alliance for Cinema and Television (PACT), registered two thousand two hundred and fifteen programmes made by independents which were commissioned and transmitted by the BBC and the ITV network. Five programmes out of those two thousand two hundred and fifteen programmes were made by black independent companies. Nought point two per cent. There's nice work around, but we're not getting it.

The BBC's twenty-five per cent independent production quota has bypassed the black independent sector. And no, it's not because we're not sending in the proposals. We are. ...

The twenty-five per cent quota has excluded black independents because it has been operated on the basis of goodwill. Goodwill does not work. Goodwill has failed black producers, directors, writers, technicians and other media professionals. Goodwill does not ensure that in these uncertain, risk-avoiding times, that commissioning editors will take a huge breath and not use those familiar names in those well-worn address books which most of the time do not feature the telephone numbers of African-Caribbean or Asian media professionals. ...

The lack of usage of the black producers and directors is directly linked to the appalling stereotypes which pass for the portrayal of black people on the screen (that is when we're on the screens at all). If we're not involved in the portrayal of ourselves, who is going to do it properly for us? ...

And nowhere is that more painful than in BBC drama. If some positive steps to end lackadaisical portrayals has been made in comedy and light entertainment, then drama is still in the dark ages. Black productions when they do get on air are concentrated in documentary.

I would urge the BBC to create a development fund specifically for the development of black drama projects. The development of projects which BBC drama heads believe have more than a passing chance of getting to air. ...

I would like the BBC to include questions in the performance appraisals of managers about how individual departments are doing with respect to the commissioning of minority programmes and the portrayal of characters from those minorities. If managers fail to take on board the need to change the white, male, middle-class, middle-aged culture that reigns at the BBC, then their pay awards should reflect this. ...

The BBC is publicly funded; publicly owned; but I do not believe it is serving its black public. Its priority for the 1990s is to get black talent on the screens and to use them behind the screens. Until that happens, it is sheer hypocritical hogwash to say that black people are members of this country. Until that happens, black people will not be part of the British landscape. (SOI Film and Television Ltd. pp. 1–2, 3, 5–6)

Privatisation of Transmission

Introduction

1. The BBC has always owned its own transmission system. Until the 1990 Broadcasting Act the transmission system for commercial television and radio was also publicly owned – by the Independent Broadcasting Authority. The 1990 Act privatised the transmission system for commercial broadcasting and it is now run by a private company, National Transcommunications Ltd (NTL). The Green Paper asks whether the BBC's transmission system should follow suit into the private sector.

Supporters of Privatisation

2. The regulators and the trade organisations of both commercial television and commercial radio are all in favour of privatisation of BBC transmission:

> Privatisation of BBC Engineering would ... provide an alternative major supplier of transmission services to *all* broadcasters and would be the best way of pursuing cost controls while at the same time maintaining standards. (AIRC, 9, p. 5)

> Transmission is an area of activity where there would, in the ITC's view, be definite benefit to be gained by separation. The hiving-off of the IBA transmission function in 1991, and its subsequent privatisation as National Transcommunications Limited (NTL), was seen at the time as the first part of a two-stage process involving the subsequent privatisation of BBC transmission. There seems no reason to doubt the judgement made by Government at the time that competition arising from privatisation of the BBC's transmission activities would provide benefits generally, and not merely to ITC licensees.

Engineering research and development is another area in which a measure of privatisation may be appropriate. The inclusion of some R&D capability with a privatised BBC transmission company would help that company develop into new markets and would provide some healthy competition to NTL in this area. (ITC, 30–1, p. 8)

The BBC's transmission services should be sold to the private sector. The new company (NewCo), along with NTL, should be regulated by OFTEL.

Ownership of sites, masts, and related equipment should be separated from provision of transmission services. Both NewCo and NTL should be required to offer access on reasonable terms to anyone wishing to supply broadcast transmission services. (ITV, 5.1, p. 16)

The Authority believes that at least the basic elements of providing a transmission service (transmitters, sites, aerials, distribution) should be separated from the main activities of the BBC and established on a fair and effective competitive basis. This would leave both BBC and commercial sectors with the ability to procure transmission services from either of two strong and capable providers, as well as from the other operators who are now beginning to address the market. Such a separation has plenty of precedents, including France, where Radio France's transmission facilities are provided by a completely separate company, Télédiffusion de France. (Radio Authority, 52, p. 17)

Opposition and Reservation
3. Opposition to privatisation comes most loudly from the industry's main trade union, but a number of other organisations also go on record against:

The BBC's transmission services have been integral to the BBC. The commitment to public service has ensured that more than 99% of the population have access to the BBC's terrestrial services. There would not have been the same incentive for the private sector to achieve such a high level of coverage. It is far from clear that the privatisation of the Independent Broadcasting Authority transmission system has produced tangible benefits for the viewing and listening public.

The BBC's transmission facilities are also responsible for the world service. In order to ensure a high quality terrestrial broadcasting service, free at the point of use, the transmission service must be maintained as an integral part of the corporate BBC.

BECTU regrets that the green paper suggests only two options for the BBC transmission system, and that it has ignored the simple and sensible option of allowing the BBC to continue this service. BECTU strongly opposes any attempt to privatise the BBC's transmission service, and suggests that consideration be given to the effect of such privatisation on the recently created National Transcommunications Ltd. (BECTU, 4, p. 9)

The NFWI views privatising any part of the BBC with apprehension, be it transmission network or research and development, because better results in terms of quality or value for money cannot be guaranteed with privatisation. (National Federation of Women's Institutes, 11.1, p. 4)

4. While not opposed to privatisation, Channel Four raises the problem that privatisation does not itself guarantee competition:

We note with interest the suggestion that the transmission services could be privatised, as happened with the former IBA's system (now NTL). As a broadcaster we, of course, would welcome any measures which increased competition in the transmission of television pictures – indeed we think that government policy should be directed towards this end. However, we would point out that privatising BBC transmission will not itself achieve this because the new company could not offer Channel 4 or ITV an alternative to NTL without a massive and prohibitive investment in a new national network of transmitters (which would in any event be wasteful). Neither the existing BBC nor NTL transmitters are presently capable on their own of transmitting more than two channels nationally. It is highly unlikely that such an investment would make business sense. A merging of the NTL and BBC transmission operations could, however, hold out the prospect of reducing costs. Although the monopoly would continue, OFTEL could ensure that NTL's customers benefited from the economies of scale through reduced tariffs. It must also be remembered that under the old duopoly of transmission systems there was considerable investment in the research and development of new television technologies to the benefit of viewers. We would hope that in considering the future of the BBC transmitters the government does not lose sight of this crucial objective. (Channel Four, 4, pp. 2–3)

5. The same problem of competition is also raised by the ITV Network Centre which proposes its own solution:

In the 1988 White Paper, 'Competition, Choice and Quality', the Government set out is ideal long-term objective: 'a regionally-based, privatised transmission system designed to promote competition, while containing certain common-carrier obligations'. The White Paper recognised that this objective could not be realised until the BBC's Charter came up for renewal in 1996. ...

ITV believes the Government's 1988 objective remains valid, and can only be achieved by the sale of the BBC transmission service to the private sector.

Privatisation alone however will not produce competition. If NewCo simply acquired the existing BBC assets and then contracted to handle BBC transmission, there would then be two private monopolies instead of one public and one private. It is difficult to imagine what the BBC would gain from this; certainly ITV's position would not be improved.

NewCo would be prevented from bidding for ITV business by NTL's ownership of the equipment used to provide the service, and NTL would be similarly restricted from bidding for BBC business. ...

It is desirable to separate the ownership of the sites, masts, aerials, etc from the provision of a transmission service. Leaving aside environmental considerations, it would be pointlessly expensive to attempt to bring in competition by allowing the building of alternative masts. There are over 1,000 sites and masts in the United Kingdom which are split roughly 50:50 between the BBC and the NTL, but are used by both organisations.

One way to achieve the 1988 objective would be to merge the BBC and NTL organisations to create a single 'infrastructure provider', owning all the sites and masts, rather like the National Grid or the proposed Railtrack Authority. This would be required to offer access to any supplier of broadcast transmission services contracted by the terrestrial broadcasters. The transmission facilities presently owned by the BBC and NTL would have to be sold to these potential suppliers.

BBC, ITV and Channel Four would then be able to choose between competing suppliers, or indeed provide their own transmission services if they felt the could do this more cheaply themselves.

The economics of economies of scale would then suggest that a single operator would emerge to provide all services on a specific site, and perhaps on all sites in a particular region.

Alternatively, BBC-NewCo and NTL could retain their existing ownership of sites, masts, etc but be required to sell their transmission operations and to act as common carriers who would provide access on reasonable terms to any transmission supplier.

If the Government is unwilling to oblige NTL to sell any of its existing assets, it could use the opportunity afforded by the development of digital technology to create competition in the industry. Both BBC-NewCo and NTL could be required to carry *new* terrestrial broadcast transmission services on reasonable terms. This would allow not only new entrants into the market but also the two existing organisations to bid against each other for the supply of new services. (ITV, 5.2–5.3 and 5.4. ii–iii, p. 17)

6. The one other obviously interested party (apart from the viewers!) in the transmission issue is NTL. Unfortunately NTL is the only organisation responding to the Green Paper (to our knowledge) that refuses to make public its response. In a letter to the editors NTL summarises its position as follows:

> In summary then, we believe that either BBC transmission should be kept within the BBC or privatised in common ownership with NTL. The combination of BBC transmission and NTL would achieve economies of scale and modification to the existing transmission tariff would be needed. Combination of BBC and NTL transmission infrastructures would give major impetus in the liberalisation of telecommunications services in the UK. BBC Research and Development should be kept-in house and focused on supporting the BBC's business needs. (NTL letter to Peter Goodwin, 4 August 1993, p. 2)

Setting the Level of the Licence Fee

Introduction

1. Although the licence fee commands virtually universal assent as the best (or least worst) method of funding the BBC, the important question still remains at what level should the licence fee be set? A number of responses devoted particular attention to this issue. They fall into two groups.

Increasing the Licence Fee

2. A number of respondents focused on the current level of the licence fee. All who did this took the view that it was too low, and needed to rise faster than the general level of inflation:

> The BBC should be properly funded through a continued licence fee. The present licence fee corresponds neither to the amount needed for the BBC to be able to discharge all that is expected of it, nor to the value which viewers and listeners attach to the BBC. The depressed level of the licence fee is the cause of pressure on the Corporation to find savings and increase efficiency. The BBC has responded to this pressure by reducing staff numbers, closing down production resources, creating new structures, such as Producer Choice, to encourage financial accountability and cutting programme budgets. It is also disposing of properties and looking at ways of streamlining its central services and overheads.
>
> In a first instance, restructuring inevitably gives rise to additional costs. In the longer term, the BBC may be judged to be insufficiently well-resourced to meet all the objectives which have been set for it and which it has set for itself, such as long-term investment in technologies, research and development, and training. Insofar as the BBC continues to be almost totally reliant on the licence fee, the level of the licence fee and the procedures for

reviewing it should be such that the BBC can budget effectively for the full range of its activities. (BSAC, p. 1)

Because increased competition will continue to drive up the cost of high quality and popular programming, the BBC requires licence fee increases which go beyond increases in the Retail Price Index and any growth in GNP. It needs 'RPI and GNP Plus' formula. (City University, Communications Policy Research Unit, 1, p. 2)

The facts and figures section of the green paper supports the view that for 22p a day the licence fee offers exceptionally good value for money. In real terms the effect of the government's decisions in the last five years has been a reduction in licence fee income. The financial crisis that this has created is self-evident. A high quality public broadcasting service costs money, and the government decision to reduce the BBC's income has undoubtedly damaged the BBC's output.

It is unreasonable and unfair for government continually to move the goal-posts in relation to the corporation's funding. There is a strong case for a modest increase in the licence fee to restore the corporation's ability to provide a wide range of high quality programme services. The corporation must be allowed to make sensible plans for the future, and to do this it must have a clear idea of its likely income over the foreseeable future. A straightforward and fair way to achieve this is to link the licence fee to the retail price index, and to ensure that this linking is honoured in real terms. (BECTU, 5, pp. 11–12)

Setting the Level
3. A second group focused on the method by which the level of licence fee is determined. The Consumer's Association outlined some of the problems:

... it should certainly not be assumed that viewers would necessarily welcome a real cut in the licence fee if this meant a cut in the quality and range of programmes on offer. The Green Paper has confirmed that following the 3% real cut in April 1991

'the Government intends to keep further increases until 1996 in line with the RPI, subject to a mid-term review of the BBC's progress with measures to improve efficiency and to generate revenue.'

Extending Choice (page 31)

This is all very well so far as it goes, but it leaves a lot of questions unanswered. In particular, we are concerned that the Government does not seem to have learned enough from the now extensive experience of price controls in the public utilities, which has increasingly highlighted the following issues:

(i)   *Is the RPI the best measure?* The Index may represent the burden on the 'typical household', but it does not necessarily reflect the costs faced by a particular industry. Work has been done on developing alternative measures which have more meaning in the terms of the body being regulated – for example the price control formula for British Gas now uses a gas price index as well as the RPI.

(ii) *Does this kind of formula provide the right kind of incentive for the BBC to increase its efficiency?* Improved efficiency – in the form of greater output per unit of input – is clearly in the interests of viewers and listeners, but there is a risk that on its own that simply indexing the licence fee to the RPI will be treated as a justification for 'cost-plus' budgets that merely reflect those of the previous year plus an allowance for inflation. There ought to be an incentive to improve services on offer.

(iii) *Does the BBC have the right output measures?* Efficient regulation ought to provide a clear incentive for the organisation to achieve a specified target – in the case of public utilities, this is increasingly being done by including a quality of service variable which reduces permitted price increases if services do not match up to what is required. In contrast, the BBC has not been told the precise standards which it is expected to achieve if it is continuing to receive increases in its licence fee. The Green Paper does propose (on page 35) the use of performance measures, though these are to be established and monitored by the BBC itself and will not be linked to the level of the licence fee. An independently monitored formal price control for the BBC could be very effective – but it needs to be much more sophisticated than that currently envisaged.

This last point also raises questions about who should be monitoring the BBC's performance. (Consumers' Association, 5b, pp. 8–9)

4. Consultants Arthur Andersen argued that their proposed single broadcasting regulator should set the level:

The level of funding should be reviewed by a body independent of the Government which would submit its recommendations to Parliament. It should be based on discussions between the BBC and the regulatory body about the BBC's objectives and targets. This is not dissimilar to the way the public utility companies are regulated.

The BBC would present a five-year plan to the regulator to set the approximate level of funding over that period. This would allow the BBC to plan in the medium term on the basis of a fixed revenue stream. Annually, the BBC would present its plans for allocation of that funding to meet its public service broadcasting objectives. The regulator would review the BBC's performance against its objectives and determine any changes in the level of funding. The regulator would recommend the BBC's level of funding to Parliament. (Arthur Andersen, p. 21)

5. Both the Labour Party and PACT linked the two issues of level of funding and method of settling it:

The present Government has effectively reduced the BBC's real income, first by holding the increase below the Retail Price Index (RPI), and now by insisting that it remains in line with the RPI until 1996, ignoring the fact that broadcasting costs have risen ahead of the index.

This 'squeeze' following the 1986 Peacock Report into the financing of the BBC has been seen as a form of direct pressure on the BBC to comply with the Government's enthusiasm for a reduction in the size and scope of the Corporation. The BBC's latest response has been to develop a medium-term strategy based upon the assumption that the real value of the licence fee will continue to fall, along with its 'market share'. On each occasion this has meant deep cuts.

On the whole issue of funding and the licence fee, it is clearly important that the BBC's independence from government should be made real and as transparent as possible – and that the BBC is allowed more confidence and flexibility in long-term planning. Equally, however, it is clear that the government will always be concerned about the impact, on those who will have to pay, of any changes to the licence fee. We are therefore examining a number of options on how best to strike a fair balance between these and other considerations. These options include, for example, the appointment of an independent Review Body to make recommendations to the Government; and the possibility of index-linking the licence fee over, say, a ten year period. We would welcome comments and evidence on these points. (Labour Party, 5.06–5.08, pp. 21–2)

... the BBC has been running down its operating reserves in order to finance new production over the last few years and the licence fee must actually be enhanced if the BBC is to enhance current levels of new production and pursue all its existing public service objectives.

The final suggestion in this paper cannot be represented as adopted PACT policy. It is, however, one that has been floated by some independents, and may be of interest to the Government.

If the Government concludes, as we hope it will, that the licence fee continues to be the best means of raising the funds necessary to sustain the BBC, it will then consider what should be the mechanism for setting, from time to time, the level of that fee. The traditional mechanism of Parliamentary vote, is unsatisfactory, in that Parliament has no real ability to assess the BBC's financial needs, to measure its performance in applying the funds voted to it, or to judge the degree to which the BBC is satisfying the expectations of licence payers.

This suggestion draws on experience of the regulatory and consumer-protection bodies created by legislation over the last decade and more as previously public utilities have been transferred to the private sector. OFWAT, OFTEL, OFGAS, OFFER, etc.

Might it be more acceptable to the public and to Government for the BBC to be given the responsibility for setting its own 'price', subject to the scrutiny and agreement of an independent body of the consumer?

We do not suggest that such a body should enjoy the full regulatory powers of an OFWAT or OFGAS – that is for the Governors; but it should be endowed with sufficient resources to enable it to set (and from time to time to revise) performance indicators for the BBC, in terms both of the range and quality of its various services and of the efficiency with which it delivers them, and to commission the research and other work necessary to monitor the BBC's adherence to those indicators.

We offer this idea to the Government as just that: an idea, rather than a firm recommendation. (PACT, 8, pp. 13–14)

The Legal Framework of Charter Renewal

Introduction

1. Throughout this book we have tended to assume, along with most of the other participants in the debate, that what was under discussion in terms of the future of the BBC is, in legal terms, the renewal of the Royal Charter under which the BBC has always conducted its affairs. However, a number of responses argued that such a legal framework for the BBC is no longer right.

2. The Labour Party outlined the shortcomings of the Charter:

> When the Crawford Committee reported in 1926, its preferred options for the future management and control of broadcasting were those favoured by the BBC – the creation of a public corporation under statute or the Companies Act. The decision to establish it as a public corporation under Royal Charter in 1927 was an acknowledgement of the monopoly it held at the time by virtue of Government licence. The Charter gave the Corporation status and dignity, the appearance of independence from Government, and considerable freedom to develop in what were then uncharted waters.
>
> Since then the Charter has been renewed periodically after discussion between the BBC and the Government. The Charter is laid before Parliament as a courtesy, but is not subject to parliamentary approval, and MPs are asked to approve, without amendment, the Licence and Agreement which permit the BBC to broadcast.
>
> This process could be considered inappropriate to a modern democracy. While the public may be asked its views on the BBC's future, their elected representatives are barred from any meaningful say over the Charter's content and play no part in the appointment of the Board of Governors. In recent years there has been increasing evidence that appointments to such major public bodies

are made on party political grounds, reversing convention that membership should be broadly representative.

Circumstances have changed dramatically since then. The accommodation of commercial broadcasting was accomplished by Act of Parliament, and it has become clear that a Royal Charter confers an unacceptably high level of discretion upon the Government. (Labour Party, 1.18–1.21, pp. 6–7)

An Act of Parliament
3. The Party went on to argue that serious consideration therefore had to be given to renewing the foundation of the BBC by Act of Parliament:

One option for the future of the BBC that deserves investigation is the possibility of renewing its Charter, Licence and Agreement by means of an Act of Parliament. This would require the Government to publish its proposals in a White Paper for public discussion, followed by detailed debate of a Bill in Parliament. *It would not preclude the granting of a Royal Charter as part of the statute.*

The parliamentary process could also facilitate amendment of the discredited Broadcasting Act 1990 to the benefit of the viewing and listening public and the broadcasting industry.

The Labour Party would welcome wide public discussion of the advantages and disadvantages of defining the BBC's function by *statute*, an approach that has never been fully explored. *The central issue is that the BBC's independence must be strengthened, not compromised, and politicians must not be allowed to control the BBC.* (Labour Party, 1.23–1.25, p. 7)

4. Two other respondents also argued for an Act of Parliament:

When the BBC was first incorporated a Royal Charter may have been the right instrument. Since then, however, the practice has developed of conventional legislation to regulate independent broadcasting; and public and Parliamentary interest in the governance of the BBC has grown greatly. In today's circumstances the balance of argument appears to lie in the use of a conventional Act of Parliament to replace the Charter. This would have the advantage of allowing Parliament to debate, and if necessary amend, the detail of the legislation in draft form.

It is argued that only a Charter can protect the BBC against undesirable day to day interference from Government and

Parliament. But, in fact, non-interference depends more upon well-established convention than upon the form of the Charter; and pressures on Parliamentary time should supply a sufficient safeguard against over-frequent legislation. (Radio Authority, 88–9, p. 26)

It is our view that the BBC should be founded on an Act of Parliament, as is the rest of the broadcasting system, and not on a Royal Charter. This would be a significant step towards democratising the debate on public service broadcasting in the UK. (Campaign for Press and Broadcasting Freedom, 4.1, p. 3)

Other Issues

Introduction

1. Most organisations responding to the Green Paper indulged in at least some fairly obvious special pleading. And many points were only discussed in detail by one or a handful of organisations. In either case the issues raised are unlikely to prove as central to the debate around the future of the BBC as the major points of controversy we have highlighted in the previous chapters. That does not mean that they are unimportant. We give below a selection of some of these other points.

Children

2. Many organisations referred in passing to the importance of the BBC's children's programming. The single in-depth response on this subject came from British Action for Children's Television:

> BACTV welcomes the likely extension of choice for children through satellite or cable services but does not believe that these can be seen as any real substitute for the terrestrially provided services of which the BBC is a cornerstone. Evidence suggests that these new services will concentrate upon entertainment programming, for the most part aimed at a general child audience. It is likely that much of the programming will be imported and that little funding will be available for home produced quality programmes. We believe that many of the long recognised arguments for public service broadcasting remain, and apply particularly to provision for children. ...
>
> We would have some concern about the BBC's emphasis on both classic plays and classic literary adaptations within its proposals for adult drama if this philosophy were also to be applied to children's output. Whilst BACTV would fully endorse the value

of having classic adaptations of children's books as an important element in children's programming ... we believe it is equally important that the drama offered young people should reflect contemporary experience. Whilst 'soap operas' such as 'Grange Hill' offer one such strand, it will be crucial for the BBC to continue to invest in shorter serials or series which can explore a wide range of situations relevant to children of different ages. We would also like to see a continuing commitment to original drama for children as well as to adaptations from children's books: ...

Extending Choice rightly draws attention to the changing nature of British society (p. 9) and it is essential that any aspiration for the BBC to help shape national culture should take this increasing variation into account. This means offering children the chance to experience differing attitudes and situations, rather than assuming any false homogeneity. It will also mean continuing to enable children to approach difficult areas of human experience through both drama and factual programming. This, too, is part of a proper public service remit, rather than any tendency to go for 'safe' subjects or sentimental treatments which might seek to shelter children in an artificially safe and anodyne television haven (which sometimes seems a characteristic of some older imported drama for children to be found on our screens). (British Action for Children's Television, 2.2, 2.13–2.14)

Religion

3. Several Christian organisations responded to the Green Paper although the majority devoted most of their attention to matters other than religious programming. One specific criticism of the BBC's approach to religious broadcasting came from the Church of England's Communications Committee:

The perennial questions about the meaning of life are always with us. While these questions are raised in many different programme formats, they are focused most sharply in religious broadcasting. Indeed, it is impossible to understand British culture without the role played by religious belief and practice in the life of these islands. It is strange, therefore, that in 'Extending Choice' the BBC includes religious broadcasting in its educational output, as something to be learned about, rather than placing it in the category of culture as something which informs the whole. Given the growth of Britain as a pluralist society, it is important that religious broadcasting continues to celebrate, affirm, explain and propagate religious belief, accepting that this is predominantly Christian,

116

though not exclusively so. These programmes should continue to be scheduled when a major audience is available. The percentage of airtime devoted to religious programmes, particularly on television, does not adequately reflect the level of interest in spiritual matters in the population, nor does it meet sufficiently the needs of communities of faith. There should be a substantial increase in religious broadcasting, both locally and nationally, which should be properly equipped and adequately resourced, to provide a range of religious programming. (Church of England Communications Committee, 10, pp. 2–3)

4. The Union of Muslim Organisations of UK and Eire brought attention to what it saw as the weaknesses of the BBC's treatment of Islam:

... in order to ensure diversity and choice, the BBC has to recognise the present reality of this country being multi-racial and multi-religious and transmit sufficient programmes about the racial and religious minorities which will cater to their needs as well as being of educational value to the indigenous population.

Our main complaint is that there are not sufficient programmes on Islam, let alone on prime time, although there are over two million Muslims living in this country and over one and a quarter billion worldwide. When some programmes on Islam are transmitted they do not properly reflect the true perspective of Islam, either through a lack of knowledge by the producer or by soliciting advice from Muslims who do not possess the requisite qualifications to do so. Our Union (UMO) is the representative body of the Muslim community in this country but we are not being consulted about any Islamic programmes nor is our representative on the Board of Governors of the BBC. We do subscribe to the principle of editorial independence but this should not be used to mislead the audiences by a wrong portrayal of the factual content or the moral implication of a programme particularly dealing with a religious subject. (Union of Muslim Organisations of UK and Eire, pp. 1–2)

Science
5. It is a revealing fact about British culture that the BBC's treatment of science scarcely figured in the great majority of responses. There was, however, one notable exception:

In a developed society, science and technology affect almost all aspects of daily life at home and at work. As this dependence progresses, and if we are to consider ourselves as truly cultured, a broad awareness of science and technology issues is essential throughout the population. ...

As the most powerful means of communication, broadcasting plays a key role in informing the public. Good quality science and technology programmes exist on radio and television, but their quantity and breadth (in terms of audience) and therefore impact is limited. In general, broadcasters' interpretations of science and technology are too narrow, the issues portrayed as difficult and the programmes relegated to specialist status.

What is needed is a commitment to support the development of innovative, novel and balanced forms of programming – including science and technology – throughout all broadcasting strands and appealing to all groups of the population. ...

The quality of the BBC's science and technology programming is well established and recognized worldwide as second to none. It provides an important seedbed both nationally and globally and should be encouraged to continue to build upon its reputation. Quality science and technology programming of this kind depends upon an internal core of specialists with the necessary skills and experience to ensure the best use of available resources. The BBC currently has such a core and is adequately placed to illustrate good science and technology programming in all parts of the country, in both the nationalized and privatized sector. For this reason it should set a precedent to maintain a staff body of some substance capable of providing the reservoir of expertise and experience which is required to identify and communicate scientific and technological ideas in a format and to a standard which satisfies public demand.

One specific issue which needs consideration is the total separation between science and technology specialists and those who are responsible for science and technology in other departments, such as news and current affairs. This divide must be eliminated and special attention paid to interchange and regular liaison between staff from the different departments. The benefits of collaboration are mutual. Science and technology stories may be compartmentalized but at least they usually contain cross-references to social or economic implications. The reverse is rarely true and it is essential that this balance should be redressed. It is particularly important to integrate with other cultural programmes and to make use of the chance to generate new interests by providing viewers with the opportunity to come into contact with information and culture they may not previously have been aware of.

In order for these principles to be firmly built into public service broadcasting, COPUS considers that the new BBC Charter should take account of the following:

(a) the new Charter should specifically require the BBC to raise the public's awareness of science and technology issues, and
(b) this obligation should be recognized and supported in any revised funding arrangements. (Committee on the Public Understanding of Science, pp. 1–3)

Education

6. A number of organisations concerned with education responded to the Green Paper. They were generally very supportive of the BBC. Several specific issues concerned with education are worth particular note.

The Adult Literacy and Basic Skills Unit (ALBSU) emphasised the BBC's role in basic literacy and numeracy:

We recognise ... the continued development of satellite and cable channels and the increased access of many people to a wider range of television and radio programmes. We believe that the BBC will continue to be in a unique position as a national broadcaster. The Corporation has a significant contribution to make in reaching a large number of people. ...

Continuing education programming should be concerned with areas of clear national priority. For instance, the BBC should be involved in helping to meet the National Education and Training Targets and with ensuring that citizens acquire a minimum standard of educational competence. Other education topics which usually attract a motivated and informed audience, such as craft, cookery and leisure programmes are better suited to 'narrow casting' and should be left to dedicated satellite and cable broadcasters.

Some education programmes, particularly those intended to motivate, should be transmitted during 'peak time' on BBC1. Increasingly education programmes have been consigned to 'non-peak' slots and have been little more than 'narrow cast' for dedicated audiences. Motivational programmes should include very brief announcements between regular programmes and continuing education needs to be given regular access to peak time continuity slots. ...

The quality of basic skills programming produced by the BBC has been variable. Some has been excellent; too much has, however, been of poor quality with low production values. We believe that this is largely because of the undiluted control BBC producers and other staff have over programme content and the difficulty faced by a specialist body such as ALBSU in gaining influence.

We believe that education programmes aimed at 'non-traditional' participants in post-school education and training need to involve the most creative production staff. There is, in our view, a case for putting most education programmes 'to tender' both to independent production companies and to different departments within the BBC. We are not convinced that employing a large number of producers who work only in continuing education is justified; nor do we believe that continuing education attracts, on the whole, the most talented and creative production staff. (Adult Literacy and Basic Skills Unit, 12, 14–15, 17–18, pp. 3–4)

7. The BFI emphasised the BBC's potential and responsibility in media education:

We would like to see the BBC's public role extended to include support for education about the media. One of the BBC's primary roles is to educate through all its programming. People learn about social groups, moral issues and critical attitudes through entertainment and drama as much as through programmes which have an explicit educational aim. Education about the media itself is an extension of the BBC's public service remit and should entail a critical engagement with all modern media. The need of all citizens to understand and interrogate the output of television and radio has never been greater and the BBC should ensure adequate provision of high quality educational materials about the media.

In this respect it is important that the BBC's educative functions are linked to other governmental, educational and cultural institutions and bodies concerned with education about the media. Improving access to understanding and production of the media should be actively promoted not only through such outlets as BBC Schools, regional broadcasting, adult education and media education in the formal education system but also reflected in the BBC's policies and programmes. The BBC's role is to recognise the importance of media education and to collaborate with those who seek to provide it. (British Film Institute, p. 7)

8. In the field of schools programming the responses revealed a dispute on the issue of night-time downloading. A majority of those who discussed the issue opposed moves to push more schools broadcasting into night-time:

Since the early 1980s, the BBC has followed a policy of putting out Schools Radio at night. The initial result of this was a fall in audience of about 50% and, although this was later reversed, the audience never fully recovered. In 'Extending Choice' (page 37) there is a suggestion that there will be an increase in this policy for all Schools Radio and TV. This we regard as a retrograde step which will probably result in another audience decline and is therefore a potential threat to the service as a whole. Many schools, both for security and insurance reasons, cannot leave equipment switched on over night. However, and probably more importantly, this isolation of schools broadcasts into a night-time ghetto devalues their general appeal and deprives parents, and other interested people, of the opportunity of listening to what their children are hearing at school. They cannot, therefore, take an active interest in this aspect of their children's education. This is at a time when the Government is pressing for more and more participation by parents in school life. (Geographical Association, pp. 4–5)

9. However, at least one respondent was in favour of downloading and made proposals as to how to use it more effectively:

Two major developments have significantly and beneficially changed the *use* of schools television broadcasts in the last five years. Firstly, the widespread availability of VHS video recorders (VCR) has led to a rapid decrease in the number of classes using broadcasts live off-air. Secondly, with the implementation of the National Curriculum, teachers now *select* broadcast material more carefully alongside other resources to support the work that they have planned. However, despite these changes, the pattern of transmission of schools broadcasts has changed very little. As a result teachers have to continue to accommodate a broadcasting system essentially designed for more leisurely times when recording equipment was rare in schools and programmes were generally heard or viewed 'live', in their entirety and without interruption.

Making selections from broadcasts implies being able to draw on a range of programme material. Weekly transmission of the individual programmes in a series not only creates extreme difficulties in making a complete set of recordings but it also inhibits or delays the selection process. In those schools without technical help, making recordings of weekly broadcasts is invariably a chore fraught with difficulties. Primary schools, in particular, frequently have extremely complex timetables for recording and playback because often there is only one VCR available. ...

While a few programmes of a topical nature and some of those intended for young pupils might be better broadcast on a regular weekly basis, NCET has no doubt that the transmission of schools broadcasts in blocks of, say, five programmes in sequence would be preferred by most schools. This would result in better quality recordings having precise starts and finishes, with no extraneous distracting material between the programmes, and most important, all the programmes of a series on one tape. It would also reduce the major complications experienced by schools in organising recordings.

Undoubtedly, many schools would like block transmissions of schools programmes in the daytime. NCET recognises that one of the principal reasons for not providing this service lies in the BBC's wish to protect the interests of home viewers. We question, however, the validity of this argument because we have not been able to find evidence to suggest that there are consistently large numbers of regular home viewers for individual schools broadcasts. ...

The night-time block transmissions of schools television might well prove to be a feasible means of delivering the service in the longer term. However, schools and colleges would need time to equip and adjust to this type of service. When unsupervised recording are made, the reliability of scheduled timings becomes critical. There is much to be said for the provision of electronic devices to switch on video recorders remotely via a transmitted coded signal. ...

It is not straightforward to find items on a videotape without proper indexing – NCET considers this to be a major weakness of schools television. Broadcasters could do much to help by transmitting a 'contents page' at the start of each programme or series, similar to that already provided for programmes on BBC Select. If this gave the duration of each programme section it would enable teachers to plan and locate easily the parts they wanted to use. (National Council for Educational Technology, 6–8, 10–12, pp. 4–5)

Film

10. The BFI argues that the BBC has a responsibility towards the health of British cinema:

The BFI is particularly concerned to ensure BBC involvement in a coherent strategy to sustain and revivify the British film industry. Its investment strategy of recent years into British film, with such notable successes as *Truly, Madly, Deeply* and *Enchanted April,* has to be capitalised upon, and the BBC encouraged to invest in other aspects of UK cinema. We would like to see greater involvement by the BBC in the funding of cinema film ... and to ensuring that such films have a cinema exhibition life before they are played on TV. The BBC also should have a duty to ensure that their patronage is made available in other aspects of the film culture. In many other European countries, comparable broadcasting organisations would either be taxed for the benefit of cinema film production, distribution and exhibition, or else statutorily required to fund many such aspects of the cinema film industry. (British Film Institute, pp. 6–7)

HDTV

11. ITV points to one key technological development missing from the Green Paper:

The Green Paper does not discuss High Definition Television (HDTV): yet, within a few years of the BBC's Charter being renewed in 1996, HDTV will be a major new broadcasting opportunity.

HDTV is 1250-line television – double the existing PAL-signal. It produces pictures of great quality. It may well be possible to transmit such pictures before 1996: however the display technology needed to make HDTV sets a commercial proposition is not as well advanced at the moment. It could however be a reality by the end of the decade, certainly within the period of the next BBC Charter.

The Government ought therefore to address the implications of this development. In the USA the Federal Communications Commission has already developed public policy on HDTV. The FCC propose that the US terrestrial broadcasters be allocated the additional spectrum needed to deliver a 'simulcast' HDTV service alongside their existing services, as part of a plan to convert all viewing to HDTV over a period of 15 years.

ITV believes that a similar policy would be appropriate in the United Kingdom, and asks the Government to begin consultations on this issue in order to include appropriate provisions in the 1995 legislation. (ITV, 6, p. 18)

Training

12. The importance of the BBC as the most significant provider of training in broadcasting is touched on in many responses. The two below deal at rather greater length (and from somewhat different

perspectives) with how the BBC's training should fit into the larger and changing training environment:

One advantage of the scale of the BBC in its integrated form is that it can offer the range of employment and career development opportunities which smaller broadcasting operations cannot generally provide. Although an increasing number of BBC programmes are being made by independent producers, the scale of in-house production still involves large numbers of creative and technical support staff. The BBC has always been a magnet for people wanting to work in broadcasting, and its formal training programmes deservedly have a strong reputation. The BBC's training effort has always been regarded as an asset for UK broadcasting as a whole, and it should be continued on that basis.

ITV and Channel 4 already contribute to training, both directly through courses they run and indirectly through financial contributions to bodies such as the National Film and Television School. These courses and contributions, which are often addressed to meeting the specific needs of the commercial sector, should continue. However there may be scope for the BBC's training services to be more open for use by non-BBC broadcasters, on a fee paying basis, than they have been in the past. This would help to ensure that the BBC's commitment to training remains strong and broadly based. (ITC, 28–9, p. 8)

The one issue which the Green Paper does not raise is the implications of the greater dependence on freelance staff within the industry. This has implications for training. The movement of staff between sectors means that cross-sectoral initiatives in training are of paramount importance if skill levels are to be maintained.

There has to be a commitment on the part of the BBC to train not only its staff but also freelancers. With training budgets delegated to department heads the temptation will be to invest those funds in training department staff. The Charter should oblige the BBC to invest in initiatives which provide training for both its own staff and for freelancers. At regional level the regional Controller should be responsible for developing the region's training strategy and establishing a training framework for his budget-holders to work within.

In view of the increased mobility of the workforce between the sectors of the industry, the current development of National Vocational Qualifications for the industry will prove invaluable. But standardisation and harmonisation of skill level assessment do not in themselves prepare an individual for the different working cultures which have developed in each sector. To ensure flexibility and the capacity of the workforce to adapt to the working practices of each sector of the industry where they may be required to work TAC comes down firmly in favour of cross-sectoral training initiatives rather than 'in-house' training.

If the BBC retains an in-house training capacity, it should not be subsidised. Its courses should be open to any purchaser of training. (TAC – The Welsh Independent Producers Association, 6.1–6.4, p. 10)

Appendix

The following is a list of organisations whose submissions in response to the Green Paper on *The Future of the BBC* were consulted in the preparation of this monograph:

Adult Literacy and Basic Skills Unit (ALBSU)
Advertising Association
Age Concern
AIRC (Association of Independent Radio Companies)
An Comunn Gaidhealach
Arthur Andersen
Arts Council
Arts Council of Northern Ireland
Association of Directors of Education in Scotland
Baptist Union of Great Britain
BECTU (Broadcasting Entertainment Cinematograph and Theatre
  Union)
British Action for Children's Television (BACTV)
British Deaf Association (BDA)
British Federation of Women Graduates
British Film Institute (BFI)
British Psychological Society
BFI Joint Broadcasting and Disability Group
British Retail Consortium
British Screen Advisory Council (BSAC)
Broadcasting Standards Council (BSC)
Broadcasting Support Services
Cable Television Association
Campaign for Press and Broadcasting Freedom (CPBF)
Campaign to Save Radio 4 Long Wave (UK)
Carlton Television

Channel Four
Church of England Communications Committee
City University (Communications Policy Research Unit)
Comataidh Telebhisein Gaidhlig
Committee on the Public Understanding of Science (COPUS)
Community Radio Association
Composers' Guild of Great Britain
Consumers' Association
Educational Broadcasting Council for Northern Ireland
Educational Broadcasting Council for Scotland
Equal Opportunities Commission (EOC)
Equity
Federation of Entertainment Unions
Freedom Association
Geographical Association
Granada Television
Guild of Television Cameramen
Heritage Broadcasting
HTV
Imperial War Museum
Incorporated Society of British Advertisers
Independent Television Commission (ITC)
Institute of Local Television
Institute of Practitioners in Advertising (IPA)
ITN
ITV Network Centre
Labour Party
Library Association
London Arts Board
Mechanical-Copyright Protection Society
Media Society
Mersey Television
Mothers' Union
Musicians' Union
National Campaign for the Arts
National Consumer Council
National Council for Educational Technology (NCET)
National Council for Voluntary Organisations
National Curriculum Council
National Federation of Women's Institutes (NFWI)
National Transcommunications Ltd (NTL) (letter only – submission
    kept confidential)
National Union of Journalists (NUJ)

National Union of Teachers (NUT)
Newspaper Society
North West Film Archive
Open University
PACT (Producers' Alliance for Cinema and Television)
Performing Rights Society
Radio Authority
Radio Clyde Holdings
Royal College of Nursing
Royal National Institute for the Blind (RNIB)
Royal National Institute for the Deaf and Deaf Broadcasting Council
Scottish Arts Council
Scottish Churches
Scottish Film Council
Scottish National Party
Scottish Secondary Teachers' Association
Secondary Heads' Association
S4C
Sheffield Hallam University
Society of Authors
SOI Film and Television Ltd
South West Arts Board
Sports Council
Sports Council for Wales
TAC (Teledwyr Annibynnol Cymru – The Association of Welsh
    Independent Producers)
Trade Union Congress
Union of Communications Workers
Union of Muslim Organisations of UK and Eire (UMO)
University of Sunderland (Steering Group of the Sunderland
    Conference, 'More than a Market Place: Independent Film and
    Video-making in the New Broadcasting Age')
Voice of the Listener and Viewer (VLV)
Wales Film Council and Wales Film and Television Archive
Welsh Language Board (Bwrdd Yr Iaith Gymraeg)
Women in Film and Television
Writers' Guild of Great Britain